MW00345065

PRAISE FOR *RECLAIM, RESTORE, AND REBUILD*

Carol has written an honest, sometimes heartbreaking account of families and their encounters with the sexual brokenness of other family members. She is a credible author because of her personal experience as a young wife and mother. But the strength of this curriculum is the strong, specific counsel she gives to these families. She is a teacher who writes with warmth, encouraging instruction, and deep insight. She is a technician who provides tools that individuals, families, and churches can use as they grow in their understanding of the complexity of the situations they face. Each reader will find this curriculum useful as a reference and practical guide for years to come. Ultimately, the emphasis on the importance of the work of the Holy Spirit in the process of growth and change and healing will prove to be the highest value of this curriculum.

—Dr. Nancy Heche, author of *The Truth Comes Out;*
co-editor of *The Complete Christian Guide to Understanding Homosexuality*

This series has been most beneficial to both JoAnn and me, as well as those within our group. The topics discussed have been just what we needed. The order in which various topics were presented has led our group into a relationship that has allowed each of us to be an encouragement to one another as together we travel this most difficult path. The lessons from this series have brought help and encouragement as we have studied, shared, cried, and prayed together. Each lesson has given us renewed strength, hope, and awareness that our heavenly Father is holding both our hands and those of our children.

—Gordon DeGraffenreid, former college professor

Carol Wagstaff knows firsthand the impact a loved one's sexual brokenness can have on your life. The range of trials and emotions are immense. Without God's help, you will never get past them. Through practical studies that are caring, nurturing, and biblically focused, this book provides a well-paved plan, making way for God to unravel those painful core matters needed for personal healing and wholeness. Anyone who has been affected by a loved one's sexual brokenness and desires a healing pathway will greatly benefit from this invaluable book.

—James E. Phelan, LCSW, Psy.D,
psychotherapist and author of *The Addictions Recovery Workbook:*
101 Practical Exercises for Individuals and Groups

When Christian families hear the announcement "I'm gay" from a loved one, they need immediate direction, reassurance, comfort, and godly wisdom. Nobody is more qualified to provide all four than Carol Wagstaff, who's been serving such families for decades now. An experienced and widely recognized voice, Carol has synthesized the lessons she's learned along the way and arranged them in a user-friendly, practical, and biblically sound tool that many families will sincerely thank God for. May this work get into the hands of the thousands upon thousands of families who need it.

—Joe Dallas, speaker;
author of *When Homosexuality Hits Home,*
The Gay Gospel: How Pro-Gay Advocates Misread the Bible,
Speaking of Homosexuality: Discussing the Issues with Kindness and Clarity,
and four other books on sexual brokenness;
co-editor of *The Complete Christian Guide to Homosexuality*

I am so thankful for Carol's honesty and her years of ministry experience, so evident in these pages. The workbook format, with spaces for personal responses, make it much easier to lead small groups. I recommend this book to churches and pastors who are looking for ways to minister to hurting individuals and families.

—Anita M. Worthen,
coauthor of *Someone I Love Is Gay*

It is hard to move forward when you, a friend, or a family member is grieving over sexual brokenness. Many of us don't know where to begin to heal. As one whose life has been redeemed from the bondage of lesbianism, I am grateful for the compassion and truth that emanate from these pages. Carol's book has practical resources that will give you, a family member, or your small group the tools that will help you move past the pain and into your purpose.

—Janet Boynes, founder and president,
Janet Boynes Ministries (janetboynesministries.com);
author of *Called Out: A Former Lesbian's Discovery of Freedom*
and *God & Sexuality: Truth and Relevance Without Compromise*

As Carol's pastor, I lived through some of her heartbreak and know the pain she endured. It was real! But out of her agonizing experiences and subsequent victories, she wrote a timely book that will help others face life with hope and determination. I am grateful for *Reclaim, Restore, and Rebuild* because for you and me and others, it just might be the instrument that opens the doors to freedom, forgiveness, and healing.

—H. B. London, Pastor to Pastor, Focus on the Family

With courage and honesty, Carol Wagstaff explores the biblical and cultural assumptions behind gender issues from an evangelical perspective. As with her personal story, this study reveals the many anxieties about God's plan for sexuality and its effect on relationships within families and churches. When faced with brokenness, the Word of God provides a road map for readers to walk with faith and grace in every situation. I highly recommend this study on your journey to wholeness.

—Pat Verbal, senior consultant of publishing and ministry resources,
The Christian Institute on Disability at Joni and Friends International Disability Center;
coauthor of *Life in the Balance: Real Families, Real Needs;*
managing editor of *Beyond Suffering Bible*

In *Reclaim, Restore, and Rebuild*, Carol Wagstaff quickly sets the stage for all that will follow in the book when she quotes 2 Timothy 3:16. That verse, taken from the apostle Paul's protégé Timothy, says Christians can learn from everything written in the Bible. As Carol shows in chapter after chapter, biblical characters like Nehemiah endured struggles just as we do. And as they followed God's leading, they overcame those struggles. In this interactive book, Carol helps readers walk alongside them in order to see ways to cope with—and even conquer—some of life's most heartbreaking trials, particularly the trials family members and friends face with a homosexual or transgender loved one.

—Denise Shick, executive director, Living Stones Ministries and Help 4 Families;
author of *My Daddy's Secret* and *Understanding Gender Confusion*

RECLAIM
RESTORE
— AND —
REBUILD

Hope for Families
Impacted by Sexual Brokenness

10 Studies
for Groups or Individuals
with Leaders Guide

RECLAIM
RESTORE
— AND —
REBUILD

Hope for Families
Impacted by Sexual Brokenness

10 Studies
for Groups or Individuals
with Leaders Guide

CAROL L. WAGSTAFF, M.A.

REDEMPTION
PRESS

© 2018 by Carol Wagstaff. All rights reserved.

Published by Redemption Press, PO Box 427, Enumclaw, WA 98022.

Toll Free (844) 2REDEEM (273-3336)

Redemption Press is honored to present this title in partnership with the author. The views expressed or implied in this work are those of the author. Redemption Press provides our imprint seal representing design excellence, creative content, and high quality production.

No part of this publication may be reproduced, stored in a retrieval system, or transmitted in any way by any means—electronic, mechanical, photocopy, recording, or otherwise—without the prior permission of the copyright holder, except as provided by USA copyright law.

All Scripture quotations, unless otherwise indicated, are taken from the Holy Bible, New International Version®, NIV®. Copyright © 1973, 1978, 1984, 2011 by Biblica, Inc.™ Used by permission of Zondervan. All rights reserved worldwide. www.zondervan.com. The "NIV" and "New International Version" are trademarks registered in the United States Patent and Trademark Office by Biblica, Inc.™

Scripture quotations marked NKJV are taken from the New King James Version®. Copyright © 1982 by Thomas Nelson. Used by permission. All rights reserved.

Scripture quotations marked AMP are taken from the Amplified® Bible (AMP), copyright © 2015 by The Lockman Foundation. Used by permission. www.Lockman.org

Scripture quotations marked MSG are from THE MESSAGE. Copyright © by Eugene H. Peterson 1993, 1994, 1995, 1996, 2000, 2001, 2002. Used by permission of NavPress. All rights reserved. Represented by Tyndale House Publishers, Inc.

Scripture quotations marked NASB are taken from the New American Standard Bible®, copyright © 1960, 1962, 1963, 1968, 1971, 1972, 1973, 1975, 1977, 1995 by The Lockman Foundation. Used by permission. www.Lockman.org

Scripture quotations marked NLT are taken from the Holy Bible, New Living Translation, copyright © 1996, 2004, 2007, 2013, 2015 by Tyndale House Foundation. Used by permission of Tyndale House Publishers, Inc., Carol Stream, Illinois 60188. All rights reserved.

Scripture quotations marked TLB are taken from The Living Bible copyright © 1971. Used by permission of Tyndale House Publishers, Inc., Carol Stream, Illinois 60188. All rights reserved.

Session 5
Denise Shick with Jerry Gramkow, *My Daddy's Secret*, Maitland, FL: Xulon Press, 2008, pp. 11-16. Selected passages reworded with author's permission.

Session 9
Robert's letter, introduction changed to third person, used by permission of Robert Lombardi.

Session 10, leaders guide
"Just Keep Planting" from *Principles for Personal Growth* by Adam Kahn (Bellevue, WA: YouMe Works, 2014, pp. 140-143). Used with the author's permission.

"Prayers for Prodigals" by B. J. Reinhard. Used with the author's permission.

ISBN 13: 978-1-63232-901-1 (Print)
978-1-63232-902-8 (ePub)
978-1-63232-903-5 (Mobi)
Library of Congress Catalog Card Number: 2017963419

ACKNOWLEDGMENTS

To the many friends whose lives have touched mine over the last twenty years through this ministry, thank you. You will see your stories in these pages. You have blessed me and taught me so much. I am deeply indebted to you.

To everyone who labored patiently beside me and gave me invaluable criticism and advice on this work in progress: Joe and Nati Ortega, Barbara Martin, Faye Ingle, Susan Rice, Anita Worthen, Pat Verbal, Paul Beals, Prudence Dancy, Bob Davies, Nancy Heche, Jana Hacker, and others I may have forgotten, thank you.

To my editors Marla Alupoaicei, Esther Attebery, and Lin Johnson, without whom this book would not exist, thank you.

To my Lord and Savior Jesus Christ, for His call to Living Stones Ministries and His faithful healing of my own heart, I shall be forever grateful. You are my King and my Lord.

CONTENTS

INTRODUCTION

"Nobody escapes being wounded. We all are wounded people, whether physically, emotionally, mentally, or spiritually. The main question is not 'How can we hide our wounds?' so we don't have to be embarrassed, but 'How can we put our woundedness in the service of others?' When our wounds cease to be a source of shame, and become a source of healing, we have become wounded healers," wrote Henri Nouwen.

Nouwen, a Dutch priest, prolific writer, and inspirational spiritual guide, knew whereof he spoke because he experienced same-sex attractions throughout his life. Yet no one knew of his struggles until after his death when his personal journals were opened. No evidence was found that he ever broke his vow of chastity. To God's glory, he was able to live above his woundedness and channel his life into a fruitful ministry to others.

Is it possible that this is God's plan for each of us who have been wounded? Are we, like Nouwen, called to become wounded healers? How can we take life's deepest wounds and turn them into ministry? Let me encourage you by sharing my journey.

My Story

As the daughter of a holiness minister, my mind and heart were immersed in church as far back as I can remember. A sensitive child, I accepted Jesus as my Savior at an early age and felt God's call to missions. In my childish mind, salvation depended on how well one kept the church rules. I strove to please God, my parents, and others, playing the role of a perfect little girl. My devotion and subsequent perfectionistic behavior earned me the name Goodie Two Shoes from my peers.

My Christian-college years provided wonderful friends and a future husband. It was there I met a talented, witty, youth-pastor-to-be. John,* a campus leader, was popular due to his great sense of humor. He also was called to ministry, which matched my heart's call. I envisioned the

---

* Names have been changed to protect the privacy of individuals.

two of us accomplishing great things for God. We married shortly after graduation, and I taught school while he attended seminary. While there, a beautiful son was born to us.

After his ministerial training, John accepted an invitation to serve as a youth pastor in a growing church. The senior pastor referred to him as Pied Piper because the teens adored him. Together we loved and nurtured young men and women. To the outside world, we were the perfect couple.

Behind closed doors, our relationship was strained. Intimacy was difficult, and we sought counseling with three different therapists over a four-year period. John never admitted he struggled with same-sex attraction. Dr. Hatten*, our last counselor, finally gave up, stating he could no longer help us. John told me, "I want to do it myself."

Six months later, John was arrested and jailed. The pastor and a Christian attorney intervened with authorities to release him. That night he came home and told me, "I was arrested for being caught in a homosexual act with a minor." When I asked him if the charge was true, he said, "I wasn't doing anything wrong."

The senior pastor and church leaders tried to help him, but he seemed done with counseling. When he became involved with a handsome college student, the church took action and revoked his position as youth pastor. We were given five days to pack our belongings and leave town.

Respected leaders in the church told me, "Move on with your life. Homosexuals don't change." Our eight-year marriage ended, and I found myself alone with a six-year-old son and $600 to start over. I felt lifeless inside, like someone had buried me alive. What would I do? Where would I go?

My dreams died, and I was deeply hurt and angry at both my husband and God. Why couldn't John love me? Why didn't God answer my prayers? How could this situation be His will? Ministries to homosexuals were just getting started at that time, but I had not heard of them. Christians did not seem to know how to help people who struggled with these feelings.

Forced to begin a new life as a single mom, I moved to southern California near family. Marrying a "normal man" who could love me and be a father to my son was all I could think about. I failed to acknowledge how weak and vulnerable I was to sin. Dick*, a handsome blonde, well-to-do businessman in my church asked me out; and I was drawn by the security he afforded. A plum ripe for picking, I did not expect the outcome of our first date. Humiliated and ashamed, I could not tell anyone. Marriage seemed to be the only option. But when I approached my pastor about marrying us, he refused. "No, I won't do it. Dick is a womanizer," he said.

Dick worked a temporary job in Washington, DC, at the time, and I called him to tell him the marriage was off. He sought the advice of a pastor in the church he was attending, and the two of them struck a deal. Pastor Jeff* agreed to pay for my flight if he could not talk me into the marriage.

I flew to New Jersey to break up with Dick. "I cannot make another mistake," I told the pastor. "I cannot go through another divorce."

He replied, "Did God take care of you after your first marriage?"

I had to admit God had.

He responded, "He will take care of you whatever happens." The next day, Pastor Jeff performed our marriage. I had a knot the size of a grapefruit in my stomach.

My heart and mind were still wounded by the trauma of my first marriage—the break-up, the sudden move, the loss of my home and people we loved. In many ways, I still felt dead inside and did not care about what was happening in my life. Early in our marriage, I succumbed to the attentions of another man. I never thought I was capable of moral failure, but I underestimated the power of sin in my life.

The reality of my own unfaithfulness drove me to God's Word. How could this happen to me, Goodie Two Shoes? I reminded God, "You made me. You know what is wrong with me." For one year I read only the Bible, looking for answers. If I tried to do anything else, the Holy Spirit whispered, "If you have time to do that, you have time to read my Word."

God began to show me who I was apart from Him. The sin of self-pity dominated my life. My contaminated heart was filled with anger and unforgiveness. My critical spirit, judgmental attitudes, perfectionism, and pride only proved I was full of myself and pharisaical arrogance. He disclosed my inclination toward codependency and the worship of people instead of Him.

For the first time, I knew how much I needed God's grace—His wonderful, marvelous, matchless grace. I poured out my heart, confessed my sins, and asked God to forgive me and renew His spirit within me. He heard my prayer, and my love for God grew day by day as I continued to study the Bible. The power of God's Word transformed me, and I began a healing journey that continues to this day. My heart overflows with love and gratitude to my Lord.

God was more merciful to me than I deserved. My church invited me to serve as Director of Women's Ministries. I was especially drawn to sexually abused women, perhaps because of my own experience. Out of that class, I developed a study titled Called to Be Free, based on my study of God's Word and my healing journey. God also prompted me to study the New Age Movement that was peopled by many who identified as homosexuals or lesbians.

Four years into my ministry, Dick stopped attending church and became like a stranger to me. I resigned my position to work on our marriage. My second son was a teenager at the time, and my heart grieved that he felt the discord in our home. When the church invited me to join the staff a year later to work with senior adults, Dick agreed that I should take the job. I accepted it, thinking things were better between us.

Nine months into senior-adult ministry, I discovered Dick was involved with another woman. When I confronted him, he said, "I want to be single again."

Heartbroken, I saw our marriage of seventeen years dissolved; and I became a single mom for the second time. The timing was particularly painful. Five months before, my first husband, John, had contracted AIDS and died at the age of forty-nine.

One night I came home from work and fell on my knees, crying out to God over my broken life. How could I, as a Christian woman, have made such a mess of my life? My soul ached for answers. "Please speak to me, Lord. I don't understand why my life has turned out like this!"

I picked up my Bible and settled into my favorite chair. "Lord," I said, "I'm not going to stop reading until You speak to me." When I reached 1 Peter 2:4-5, the words pierced my heart: "As you come to him, the living Stone—rejected by men but chosen by God and precious to Him—you also, like living stones, are being built into a spiritual house to be a holy priesthood, offering spiritual sacrifices acceptable to God through Jesus Christ" (NIV84). The "living Stone" referred to Jesus, and He was "rejected by men but chosen by God." Could He understand how my heart and mind ached with rejection and shame? Was it possible that I, too, could be chosen?

The pieces of my life puzzle started fitting together. If I had not endured rejection and deep wounding, I wouldn't comprehend how individuals and families feel when sexual brokenness invades their lives and homes. God had to break my pride, my haughty attitudes, my holier-than-thou outlook and bring me to a place of humility. My life experiences showed me I was no better than anyone who had committed sin of any kind.

The church was gracious and allowed me to remain in ministry as I continued to seek the Lord's will for my life. The senior adults whom I served surrounded me with love and encouragement. God blessed me daily and taught me so much! The pain of my life seemed so small compared to the incredible joy and blessing I found in Jesus Christ. Praise filled my heart for the trials and afflictions He brought me through. He used every painful situation to teach me and mature me in my walk with Him.

One morning during my devotional time, God instructed me to resign my position at the church. I had prayed specifically for a year for God's guidance and wanted to make sure I truly heard His voice. I asked Him to confirm His leading for me; and a month later, He clearly did so. Immediately, I wrote a letter of resignation and delivered it to the church. After living with my decision for a day or so, I began to doubt if I had done the right thing. My oldest son was in college; and while I owned my home, it had a healthy mortgage. How would I support myself?

A few days later, on my way to a prayer meeting, I began to weep—so much so, I didn't feel I could go in to face my friends. No one knew I had resigned, and there would be questions. Instead, I went to my office and picked up *My Utmost for His Highest*, updated edition by Oswald Chambers. I opened it to a devotional titled "Abraham's Life of Faith." This verse caught my eye: "He went out, not knowing where he was going" (Hebrews 11:8 NKJV). Chambers went on to say, "Living a life of faith means never knowing where you are being led. But it does mean loving and knowing the One who is leading." I closed the book, weeping again, but this time with joy.

God confirmed His direction for me, but I still did not know specifics. A few days later, I was on my knees, asking God to show me what I was supposed to do. As I prayed, God brought to mind a memory of a visit to an AIDS hospice in Los Angeles. A friend was deeply concerned for her son, Jim*, who was dying of AIDS. She asked me if I would mind going with her to see him. In a room full of hurting men, I shared God's love with Jim and the Good News of His willingness to forgive any sins Jim committed, no matter how big or unforgivable they seemed. He received my words and allowed me to pray with him.

I wondered if God was calling me to be a chaplain in an AIDS hospice. I got up from my knees and called the Gay and Lesbian Center in Hollywood, asking if they had any positions open for chaplains in AIDS facilities. I was told I would need to fill out an application for the volunteer chaplain's position. As I hung up the phone, God spoke clearly to me: "I want you to work with parents and family members like yourself who have been devastated by the reality of sexual brokenness in the lives of their loved ones."

I was so excited that God made His will clear to me. My friends who were praying for God's direction were among the first to know. I wrote a letter to my senior adults and read it to them the following Sunday. I still did not know how I was going to start the ministry or what to call it, but God knew. One of the men, a retired judge, approached me after my announcement and said, "Form a nonprofit, and we will support you." Another lady from my Sunday school class told me she did not want me to starve to death, and she mailed me a $20,000 check. Miracle after miracle occurred, and God continually provided for me as the ministry grew. To God's glory, He provided for me for twenty years and continues to sustain the ministry to this day.

A New Ministry

After ten years of serving on the staff of my church, God led me to begin a ministry for families with homosexual issues. Much of the wounding of my life came out of the failure of my first marriage: death of a dream, painful rejection, hurt, frustration, disappointment. The shame and guilt of two failed marriages plus my own moral failure plagued my mind and heart. I knew the trauma and long-term effects of sexual abuse. Grief was a regular visitor in my home. I watched a youth minister, whom I once deeply loved, succumb to homosexuality and death from AIDS.

God changed my heart and gave me a love for broken people, many of whom had been the target of my judgmental spirit. I learned from a psychologist friend that the key word in the homosexual world is *rejection*. I knew what it was like to be rejected, and I could identify with people who experienced it much more severely than I had. First Peter 2:4-5 fit my life, but it also fit the lives of hurting people whom God dearly loved and who needed Him. God had prepared me in unusual ways for this ministry.

Living Stones Ministries, birthed out of God's Word, defined the purpose for this new ministry. Jesus, the living Stone, was rejected but chosen and precious to God. We, too, are rejected but chosen by God and precious to Him. He desires to take our foolish choices and broken lives and build us into a spiritual house with Himself as our foundation. As we grow and mature in our faith, we become part of His holy priesthood, ministering to the wounded and broken.

God's Lessons

Through my journey, I learned:

- We can and must trust God.
- Because we are Christians does not mean we or our loved ones will not have emotional, psychological, or sexual problems.
- Performing well for the sake of others and doing good things are characteristics of a Christian lifestyle, not a vital relationship with God.
- Our families of origin and life experiences impact how we understand God and assimilate Him into our lives.
- Becoming a Christian is the easy part; working out our salvation from day to day is a lifelong pilgrimage.
- Healing is not an overnight occurrence. It is a journey, one that can take many years.
- The opposite of homosexuality is not heterosexuality; it is the pursuit of holiness.
- We need not be defined by our past or what tempts us. Our identity is in Christ. First and foremost, we are children of God.
- Peace and victory come when we cast ourselves and all our baggage on God's mercy.

Several years ago, I flew to Chicago to speak at a conference. One overcast afternoon, I visited John's graveside. I knelt on his grave marker and wept, asking God for forgiveness for being so proud, for being so judgmental, for not understanding what he had gone through. The sun broke through the clouds as I got up from my knees—a symbol of God's work in my life.

God has been more faithful and grace-giving than I ever deserved. But He is like that. He doesn't meet us where we ought to have been; He meets us where we are with real love. His grace is greater than any sin we may have committed. Praise His name!

This Book

The book you're holding was written for you. The sessions are drawn from the story of Nehemiah. While Nehemiah lived thousands of years ago, his emotions and behavior are identical to ours. He is an incredible role model because he endured so much, yet was obedient to God and fulfilled God's purposes for his life. His life reminds us that we often do not choose the circumstances God allows in our lives, but we can learn to make the best of them.

As you work through these sessions, you will see yourself and your family with new eyes. It will take courage for you to be honest and open, but growth and freedom come to those who are willing to open themselves to new truths. It is important to be receptive to meeting with a Christian counselor, pastor, or mentor to help you through the process, especially if you uncover truths that are difficult for you to bear.

Processing these sessions in a group is beneficial. Together you can work through the concepts and assist one another in gaining understanding and insight. We are healed in community; so do not give up until you find a group of people who can love you, uphold you in prayer, hear the anguish of your heart, and encourage you to grow.

Each session is built around one aspect of your journey. While this book is conveniently designed in chapter format, allow yourself the flexibility to take the study at your own pace. Let the timeline be yours in order to get the most out of each session.

As you study, don't forget God loves you, as well as your loved one who struggles with sexual brokenness. Whether your loved one is a spouse, a son or daughter, a brother or sister, Mom or Dad, or even a neighbor or friend, God's presence and guidance can give you the comfort and direction you need to survive and grow. I pray you will be able to give up your shame and, someday, become a wounded healer.

HOPE FOR YOUR JOURNEY

To all who are heartbroken and yearn for comfort:
"'As a mother comforts her child, so will I comfort you'" (Isaiah 66:13).

To all who are confused and want to know truth:
"'I, the LORD, speak the truth; I declare what is right'" (Isaiah 45:19).

To all who are discouraged and long for hope:
"'Those who hope in me will not be disappointed'" (Isaiah 49:23).

To all who feel rejected and crave love:
"'Though the mountains be shaken and the hills be removed, yet my unfailing love for you
will not be shaken nor my covenant of peace be removed'" (Isaiah 54:10).

To all who struggle with sin and hunger for God's grace:
"'I, even I, am he who blots out your transgressions, for my own sake and remembers your
sins no more'" (Isaiah 43:25).

To all who are tired and yearn for rest:
"'Come unto me, all you who are weary and burdened, and I will give you rest'"
(Matthew 11:28).

To all whose hearts are filled with fear and want courage:
"'Do not be afraid or discouraged because of this vast army. For the battle is not yours, but
God's'" (2 Chronicles 20:15).

"'"You are my servant'; I have chosen you and have not rejected you. So do not fear, for I am
with you; do not be dismayed, for I am your God. I will strengthen you and help you; I will
uphold you with my righteous right hand'" (Isaiah 41:9-10).

THE STORY OF NEHEMIAH

The Old Testament books and their stories seem so far removed from our current culture that we think we cannot relate to a society so different from our own. While the times and seasons described in the book of Nehemiah happened thousands of years ago, people still exhibit the same characteristics. No matter how we look on the outside, as human beings we experience similar thoughts, emotions, and behaviors.

So Nehemiah's story is pertinent to us. As the Bible says, "All Scripture is God-breathed [given by divine inspiration] and is profitable for instruction, for conviction [of sin], for correction [of error and restoration to obedience], for training in righteousness [learning to live in conformity to God's will, both publicly and privately—behaving honorably with personal integrity and moral courage]" (2 Timothy 3:16, AMP).

But what does God want us to learn through Nehemiah? Who was he? What do we need to know about him?

When we first meet Nehemiah, he was serving as a cupbearer in the Persian court of King Artaxerxes I. Cupbearers tasted the king's wine before he drank it to prevent him from being poisoned. The possibility of death was part of Nehemiah's daily life. Most likely, Nehemiah also was a eunuch. Male servants were made into eunuchs, deliberately castrated, so they could be trusted around the queen and other women of the court. He also became a valued and trusted advisor to the king.

Nothing is said about Nehemiah's parents. It is presumed they were taken captive by Nebuchadnezzar or killed when the Babylonians destroyed Jerusalem. (Read about the fall of Jerusalem in 2 Chronicles 36:15-21.) Jewish by heritage, he grew up as a foreigner in what is now the country of Iran. Whatever happened, we can be sure he knew the pain of being severed from his family and beloved Jewish people.

God put on Nehemiah's heart to rebuild the walls of Jerusalem, which Nebuchadnezzar destroyed in 586 BC. In ancient cities, the walls were vital, as they were the only means for people to defend their cities against their enemies. The walls symbolized strength and protection;

without strong walls, the city could not be considered safe. The city government was also located within those walls.

Nehemiah had every reason to think the job he had been given was impossible to accomplish. His contemporary, Ezra, along with the Jewish exiles, had been given permission to rebuild the temple under the reign of King Cyrus. However, much of the city still lay in ruins. When they attempted to rebuild the walls, they were stopped. The work they did accomplish on the walls was burned.

Seventy-nine years before Ezra, Zerubbabel led a group of exiles to Jerusalem in an effort to rebuild the city; but that did not happen. So God gave Nehemiah the job of rebuilding the walls, which was no small feat. City walls were often built high and thick. In the book of Daniel, we read of the massive walls around the city of Babylon, which were about 100 feet thick and 300 feet high. The coming of Nehemiah, with the blessing and help of Artaxerxes I, was God's plan for restoring His people to their homeland. God intervened in human history through Nehemiah's life. Only through God's power and guidance could the walls of Jerusalem be rebuilt in only fifty-two days.

What can we learn from Nehemiah? As you study portions of the book of Nehemiah in these sessions, you'll discover God is still in complete control and is working out the details in every life—including yours—according to His will and purpose.

1

HEARING THE NEWS

Shocking moments occur in all our lives when time seems to stand still. Mary experienced one of those moments while eating lunch with her daughter, Lisa.

"How's your job going?" Mary asked.

"It's going great, Mom. Of course, a new job always stretches us. You know the drill: adapting to new surroundings, high expectations, testy people. It's always a challenge." Lisa paused. "I really invited you to lunch today to talk about something more important."

"You mean you didn't invite me to celebrate Valentine's Day with you?" Mary's eyes twinkled. "Or to tell me you love me?"

"Oh, Mom, c'mon. Not really. You know I love you."

"What could be more important? What do you want me to know?"

Lisa took a deep breath, paused, then said, "Mom, I'm a lesbian. I thought you might know by now. Did you have any suspicions?"

Mary was stunned. She opened her mouth, but nothing came out. She wanted to reason with her daughter, but the right words wouldn't come.

After a few minutes of awkward silence, Lisa excused herself. "Why don't I call you later when you have time to think about it, Mom?"

"I don't know how I got home that day," Mary said. "For weeks I could barely eat or sleep, and I cried constantly. I couldn't help thinking that Lisa's death would have been easier to take than this announcement."

In that moment, Mary's life changed forever. She went from feeling like a good parent to feeling overwhelmed with guilt. She constantly asked herself where she had gone wrong. She desperately wanted a chance to pull her precious daughter into her arms, tell her she loved her, and correct all the parenting mistakes she had made in the past.

> "I have indeed seen the misery of my people in Egypt. I have heard them crying out . . . and I am concerned about their suffering."
> —Exodus 3:7

"The righteous cry out, and the LORD hears them; he delivers them from all their troubles. The LORD is close to the brokenhearted and saves those who are crushed in spirit."
—Psalm 34:17-18

REFLECTING

When have you received heartbreaking news about a family member or friend?

How did you respond to that news?

"You, LORD, hear the desire of the afflicted; you encourage them, and you listen to their cry."
—Psalm 10:17

EXPLORING

The biblical prophet Nehemiah was acquainted with distressing news too. He would have understood parents like Mary—and you. His heart broke over unfulfilled dreams.

1. Read Nehemiah 1:1-4. How did Nehemiah respond to the news about his beloved city?

Receiving discouraging news is painful. Its devastating effects can blindside us, especially when the news relates to someone we love and care about very much.

2. In what ways can you relate to Nehemiah's suffering?

Discovering that a family member is taking steps to embrace his or her same-sex attractions or change gender identity can be particularly devastating, especially when that person cuts him or herself off from the family. When this situation occurs, the family may feel as if that person has died. And, in truth, many of our dreams and expectations for that loved one may die.

We may find ourselves asking questions like these: Who is this person we thought we knew? How could this situation have happened to our family? What about my fervent prayers for this child or other family member? The relationship seems forever changed, perhaps irretrievably; and our faith in God and life in general may be shaken.

3. When you heard that your child or other loved one was experiencing same-sex attraction or gender confusion, how did you feel?

When our losses happen too quickly and we do not allow ourselves time to grieve, we experience *compound grief*. One loss piggybacks onto another, and we may sink into despair.

What did you say or do?

"Your word is a lamp to my feet and a light to my path."
—Psalm 119:105, NASB

4. What dreams do you have for that person?

Put the letter *D* before any of these dreams that seem to have died.

Roller Coaster of Grief

Receiving the devastating news of a loved one's same-sex attractions or gender confusion can throw us into a vicious cycle of grief. Our faith is severely tested, and our emotions take a frightening roller-coaster ride.

This cycle of emotion is predictable and intense. Shock, denial, anger, blame, depression, isolation, bargaining, panic, guilt, and mourning manifest themselves, although not necessarily in this order. Eventually, acceptance and hope are realized. (See "Stages of Grief" on page 123.)

Anticipatory grief is mourning or grieving today over future problems or the absence of a loved one.

Sexual brokenness and the negative consequences prey on our minds, and coping is difficult.

5. Which emotions are you dealing with right now?

"Though the mountains be shaken and the hills be removed, yet my unfailing love for you will not be shaken nor my covenant of peace be removed." —Isaiah 54:10

How are these emotions affecting your daily life and interactions with other people?

Compound Grief

Nehemiah was no stranger to feelings like ours. He grew up as a foreigner in a pagan country, longing for his family, his people, and his home. Memories of past atrocities experienced in Jerusalem plagued his thoughts. When new word came of the devastated condition of his city, Nehemiah mourned for days. The broken walls and burned gates brought disgrace on those he loved.

Previous losses in your life may compound your grief about your family member's sexual attractions or gender confusion. The more losses you've endured, the longer the grief cycle continues. You may wonder why you can't seem to get over this news.

If you are experiencing compound grief, your sorrow may last for an extended period of time. Be patient with yourself, remembering that God is the "God of all comfort" (2 Corinthians 1:3). He grieves with you for your loved one and will give you grace to endure one moment at a time. With His strength, eventually you can and will move on.

6. What grief experiences (e.g., death in the family, job loss, problems with another child) came along prior to the news of your loved one's same-sex attractions or gender identity issues?

How do these grief experiences influence your response?

"Though no one can go back and make a brand new start, anyone can start from now and make a brand new ending."
—Carl Bard

7. How long have you grieved over the news about your family member?

"'For I know the plans I have for you,' declares the Lord, 'plans to prosper you and not to harm you, plans to give you hope and a future.'"
—Jeremiah 29:11

Secondary Losses

8. After the initial shock of disturbing news, we may experience secondary losses. For example, a son or daughter may leave home, move in with his or her partner, or commit more fully to living as a homosexual or transgendered person. Naturally, such a decision will force changes in the family or parenting roles. What secondary losses have you experienced after the initial loss?

9. The grief cycle causes worry and fear about the future. One fear leads to another, a downward spiral begins, and the worst is expected. What trouble, shame, difficulties, or disgrace have you anticipated?

"Nothing that has occurred or will occur in heaven or earth or hell can change the tender mercies of our God. Forever His mercy stands, a boundless, overwhelming immensity of divine pity and compassion."

—A. W. Tozer

Impact of Grief

The cycle of grief paints a painful process, affecting you and your family members in physical, emotional, spiritual, and social ways. The symptoms are listed below.

Confusion	Withdrawal
Memory loss	Insomnia
Anxiety/panic	Uncontrollable weeping
Depression	Lethargy
Shame	Stomach pain
Guilt	Fatigue/exhaustion
Suicidal thoughts	Indecisiveness
Irritability	Loss of appetite
Inability to concentrate	Aggression
Nail-biting	Fear of insanity
Overwhelming anger	Frenetic activity
Excessive sleeping	Forgetfulness
Disorganization	Numbness

10. Which symptoms have you experienced during your grieving process? Underline them in the above list.

How have these symptoms impacted your life?

Beyond Grief

11. Read Lamentations 3:22–26. How did Jeremiah find relief from his grief?

Discovering a loved one struggles with same-sex attractions or gender dysphoria does not necessitate an end to the relationship. After the grieving period, we must create a new relationship with that person. When our feelings and understanding of God's truth clash with those of our loved ones, we must learn to see them through Jesus' eyes. Ask Him to show you how He sees them and how to express His love without judgment. God does not require us to agree with or approve of the lies Satan attempts to make our loved ones believe about themselves. His love is higher and greater than anything we can imagine—both for us and for them.

> "And the God of all grace, who called you to his eternal glory in Christ, after you have suffered a little while, will himself restore you and make you strong, firm and steadfast."
> —1 Peter 5:10

With regard to the heartbreak you feel about their sexual or gender issues, cast "all your anxiety on Him" (1 Peter 5:7). God knows. He cares. He understands. He loves us even while we are living in sin, and He loves your family member. You may not feel like leaning into God's arms. But staying connected to Him will make all the difference as you move through your grief.

12. How has your relationship with your loved one changed since you learned of his or her same-sex attractions or gender confusion?

13. Which elements of your relationship were not changed by this news?

14. What possibilities do you see for a new and different relationship with your loved one?

So often we're discouraged when life comes crashing around us. But don't lose heart! God is at work in your life and in your loved one's life, even in the midst of suffering.

In Philippians 1:6, the apostle Paul reminds us, "He who began a good work in you will carry it on to completion until the day of Christ Jesus." Through our pain, we're conformed to the image of Christ; and we share in the fellowship of His sufferings.

While it's important for you to keep moving forward through your grief, taking good care of *you* during this time is also vital. Here are some suggestions:

- Spend quality time with God. François Fénelon, an early Christian writer, said, "Talk with God with the thoughts that your heart is full of. . . . Tell Him without hesitation everything that comes into your head, with the simplicity and familiarity of a little child sitting on its mother's knee" (*Talking with God,* Orleans, MA: Paraclete Press, 2009, pp. 3-4).
- Ask God to give you a Bible promise to stand on for the transformation of your loved one who struggles.
- Plan recreational activities to provide a release from your stress.
- Maintain a sense of humor. (Suggestion: Read a book by Barbara Johnson, Martha Bolton, Dave Meuer, or Phil Callaway.)
- Cultivate one or more hobbies that don't involve your loved one who is encountering tough issues.
- Listen to your favorite praise music, as it will help bring you into God's presence.
- Journal your thoughts and feelings. Share them with a friend.
- Join a support group for families affected by sexual brokenness, or start one at your church.
- Learn to say no without feeling guilty.
- At bedtime each night think of at least one good thing that happened that day and praise God for it.
- Allow God to help you develop a prayer life that is not all about your loved one.

REBUILDING

God longs to "rebuild the ancient ruins and restore the places long devastated" (Isaiah 61:4).

Write a letter to God, telling Him your honest feelings about what has happened to you and your family. God is not afraid of your negative feelings. Ask Him to show you the possible good He wishes to bring out of this situation.

Memorize Jeremiah 29:11.

2

ENCOUNTERING GOD

"Do not fret because of those who are evil or be envious of those who do wrong. . . . Be still before the LORD and wait patiently for him." These words from Psalm 37 pierced Marla's aching heart. "Can I trust You, Lord?" she asked.

She laid her Bible on the coffee table and walked into the kitchen to pour another cup of her favorite chocolate-raspberry coffee. Then she remembered: Her husband, Ben, had stayed up late the night before, supposedly paying bills online. But what had he *really* been doing? The old nagging fears returned.

Marla's hands trembled as she flicked the switch on Ben's computer and turned on the monitor. She *had* to know. Before she and Ben were married, he told her he had struggled with homosexual temptations. But he promised he was past that, and she believed him. Since then, however, she caught him several times looking at pornography on the computer. Each time, he promised never to do it again.

> "Out of the depths I cry to you, LORD; LORD, hear my voice. Let your ears be attentive to my cry for mercy."
> —Psalm 130:1-2

> "Answer me when I call to you, my righteous God. Give me relief from my distress; have mercy on me and hear my prayer."
> —Psalm 4:1

Marla gasped in shock as photos of nude men flashed across the computer screen. "What is this?" she cried out in disbelief. "Not again!" She slumped in the computer chair and cried, leaning her head on the desk in despair.

"You know what, God? I'm through," she told the Lord through her tears. "I can't go on living like this! How can I keep believing in You and trusting You when I continue to get hurt this way?"

Feelings of betrayal and abandonment flooded her being, and her stomach knotted with anxiety at the thought of having to confront Ben again.

> "The Lord's mercy often rides to the door of our heart upon the black horse of affliction."
> —Charles Spurgeon

Then a still, small voice pierced her broken heart. "Marla, will you trust Me? You know My Word. Is there any part that isn't true? I've promised always to be with you."

Even in her severe emotional pain, Marla felt a slight twinge of hope. Though the journey to recovery would be difficult, she knew God would walk every step with her.

REFLECTING

In what ways does your loved one's sexual or gender issues feel like a betrayal or abandonment?

> "Consider it a sheer gift, friends, when tests and challenges come at you from all sides. You know that under pressure, your faith-life is forced into the open and shows its true colors. So don't try to get out of anything prematurely. Let it do its work so you become mature and well-developed, not deficient in any way."
> —James 1:2-4, MSG

EXPLORING

Nehemiah, too, knew what it was like to feel betrayed and abandoned by people he once trusted. Displaced by the invasion of Jerusalem and captured by people who did not honor God, he longed to return to his homeland where he could worship the Lord freely.

Processing Grief

1. Read Nehemiah 1:4-6. How did Nehemiah respond to the news about his city, family, and friends?

According to the biblical timeline, Nehemiah processed his grief before God for about four months. What happened during those months of mourning? It would seem that Nehemiah used that time to come to terms with his emotions, confess his anger, and forgive those who broke down the walls and burned the gates of his beloved city.

In our moments of desperation, especially when we hear the news of a loved one's sin and suffering, we may feel that God has deserted us. We, too, may feel like strangers in unfamiliar territory, longing for home. We may wish we could simply wave a magic wand and return everything to the way it was before.

2. The Psalmist artfully captures these feelings in the following passages. Read both passages, and write them in your own words.

Psalm 13:1–2:

Psalm 22:1–2:

Dietrich Bonhoeffer, a German theologian who was martyred for his faith, talks in his book *Life Together* about "wish dreams"—what we wish or expect should happen—in the church. We can bring these same "wish dreams" to our families and to our relationship with God.

"It is impossible to have a healthy relationship with God without having a right concept of who He is."
—Dan DeHaan

3. Which word or phrase from these two psalms best captures how you feel right now?

4. When we find out troubling news about a loved one, we may attempt to make a deal with God, saying, "God, if you will just do _____, then I will do _____. What promises have you made in exchange for the Lord's intervention in the life of your loved one?

Hearing the news about a loved one's sexual preference or gender confusion can be a terrible shock. Even if we had suspected it earlier, knowing the truth traumatizes us. We look at our loved one with new eyes; our beloved may seem like a stranger to us. We may feel as though someone has stolen away the person we thought we knew.

"Only Jesus revealed that God is a Father of incomparable tenderness, that if we take all the goodness, wisdom, and compassion of the best mothers and fathers who have ever lived, they would only be a faint shadow of the love and mercy in the heart of the redeeming God."
—Brennan Manning

5. When we are hurting, we tend to blame others for what happened. What or whom have you wanted to blame for your loved one's sexual brokenness?

6. Which aspects of your loved one have changed (e.g., personality, attitudes, actions, style of dress)?

Which aspects remain the same?

"I had passed beyond grief, beyond terror, all but beyond hope, and it was there in that wilderness that for the first time in my life I caught something of what it must be like to love God truly. It was only a glimpse, but it was like stumbling on fresh water in the desert . . . . Though God was nowhere to be clearly seen, nowhere to be clearly heard, I had to be near him."
—Frederick Buechner

Questioning God

Agonizing situations cause us to be skeptical about God. We may ask, "How could a loving God allow this to happen?" especially if we have been faithful Christian parents who did our best to raise our children to know and love the Lord with all their hearts. Aren't we entitled to a trouble-free family?

The problem with this line of thinking is that we have a limited view of God's plan. We have our own ideas about what a loving God should or shouldn't do and how He should respond to our pain. When God doesn't measure up, our faith is deeply shaken. Our anger at others may then be directed toward God.

In John 11, Martha and Mary, good friends of Jesus, were inconsolable with grief over their brother Lazarus's death. Both of them accused Jesus, "If only you had been here, my brother would not have died" (John 11:21, 32, NLT).

Like Martha and Mary, we sometimes bemoan God's seeming absence—His lack of intervention when He could have stopped a particular tragedy. But notice Jesus' response when he saw Mary's grief: "He was deeply moved in spirit and troubled. . . . Jesus wept" (vv. 33, 35). He noticed the sisters' grief. He loved Lazarus, too, and grieved his death as well.

But Jesus knew the rest of the story. He understood that Lazarus's death was simply a part of God's greater plan to reveal the Father's glory in a radical way through resurrection.

Guilt about our sin and mistakes often compounds our anger at God. "If only" we had known sooner. "If only" we had paid attention to our first suspicions. "If only" we had . . . .

7. What "if onlys" have you felt about your situation?

> "For I am convinced that neither death, nor life, nor angels, nor principalities, nor things present, nor things to come, nor powers, nor height, nor depth, nor any other created thing, will be able to separate us from the love of God, which is in Christ Jesus our Lord."
> —Romans 8:38-39, NASB

8. If God were sitting across the room from you, what would you say to Him regarding His involvement or lack of involvement in the situation?

> "'Those whom I love I rebuke and discipline. So be earnest and repent. Here I am! I stand at the door and knock. If anyone hears my voice and opens the door, I will come in and eat with that person, and they with me.'"
> —Revelation 3:19-20

9. How might your "if onlys" impact your life, especially your relationship with God?

Trusting God's Love and Sovereignty

God looks on us with infinite loving-kindness, remarkable compassion, and powerful mercy, as a father does his children. God did not create same-sex sexual attraction. He also did not create men and women in the wrong bodies, causing them to desire to change their birth gender to the opposite one. In fact, both are against His divine plan for creation; and both are against Scripture's clear teaching for human sexual behavior. The distortion of God's plan for a sacred union between a man and a woman does not glorify Him. But He still loves His children and longs to see them live in obedience to Him.

> "The forgiveness of Jesus not only takes away our sins, it makes them as if they had never been."
> —Anita Worthen

10. Read Psalm 139. What characteristics of God do you see in this chapter?

> "'As the Father has loved me, so have I loved you. Now remain in my love. If you keep my commands, you will remain in my love, just as I have kept my Father's commands and remain in his love.'"
> —John 15:9-11

11. Which verse gives you the most comfort?

Why?

God's love is immeasurable, unstoppable, uncontainable, and inexhaustible. When we experience grief and heartache, He longs for us to come to Him in prayer, so He can comfort us. His Holy Spirit moves within our hearts, reassuring us of His love.

Remember: God knows you, and He understands your loved one's personal struggles. He sees the past, the present, and the future. Nothing escapes His notice!

He reminds us, "'Do not fear, for I have redeemed you; I have summoned you by name; you are mine . . . . You are precious and honored in my sight, and . . . I love you . . . . Though the mountains be shaken and the hills be removed, yet my unfailing love for you not be shaken nor my covenant of peace be removed'" (Isaiah 43:1, 4; 54:10).

12. When we face tough situations, we have a choice to control the circumstances in our own power or to walk in faith, fully surrendered to God's will. Which one comes more naturally to you?

13. In what ways have you tried to change or control your loved one's feelings or behavior?

What were the results?

> "Trust in the Lord with all your heart and do not lean on your own understanding. In all your ways acknowledge Him, and He will make your paths straight."
> —Proverbs 3:5-6, NASB

We can trust God because we know Jesus. The author of Hebrews tells us, "The Son [Jesus] is the radiance of God's glory and the exact representation of his being, sustaining all things by his powerful Word" (1:3). We can plainly see and experience God's incredible love by knowing Jesus, who became a man in order to live on Earth and die a sacrificial death on the cross to redeem us from our sins. Then He rose again to conquer death and purchase a place for us in God's eternal Kingdom.

Having Jesus in your life while you deal with the pain of your loved one's homosexuality can offer you comfort, stability, peace, and the knowledge that He is in control. If you have never committed your life to Jesus, please consider doing so. If you're not certain how to do it, you can pray the following prayer:

> *Dear Jesus,*
> *I need you! I confess I have been trying to run my life on my own, and I ask you to forgive me. Please come into my heart and reign on the throne of my life. Thank you for dying on the cross for my sin. Thank you for forgiving me and giving me the gift of eternal life. I commit to serving you with all my heart.*
> *In Jesus' name, amen.*

When we establish a relationship with God by accepting Jesus as our personal Savior, we have the greatest power in all the universe available to us. It's no wonder Nehemiah called God "the great and awesome God, who keeps his covenant of love with those who love Him and keep his commandments" (1:5). Nehemiah knew firsthand how good God was at loving His suffering children.

If you have already committed your life to Christ, you may want to recommit your life and this situation to Him, knowing He is sovereign and He loves you.

REBUILDING

Take time this week to ask God to renew your trust in Him. Choose at least one relevant Bible passage you can memorize and cling to as you seek wisdom and healing for your family. Write this verse on an index card, and carry it with you to review in difficult moments.

Also memorize Psalm 4:1.

3

EXAMINING OUR GUILT

After I had finished a speaking engagement at a women's retreat along the northern California coast, Carrie, a woman in her 40s, approached me and asked if I would meet with her alone. When we met at dusk, the waves lapped gently against the shore; and a fresh breeze graced us with the exhilarating scent of the Pacific Ocean. We approached a worn, wooden bench and sat down.

Slowly, Carrie confided to me her anguish over her gay son. As we continued to talk, her words and emotions surged like a powerful ocean current.

I put my arms around her as her shoulders heaved with wracking sobs. "I tried my best to be a good mother and to do everything right. I didn't realize how much my divorce would hurt him. He was so hungry for male attention! I'm sure that's why he was molested, which eventually led him to embrace this lifestyle. I wish I could go back in time and do things over again!"

> "My guilt has overwhelmed me like a burden too heavy to bear."
> —Psalm 38:4

> "As we come to grips with our own selfishness and stupidity, we . . . accept that we are impoverished and broken and realize that, if we were not, we would be God."
> —Brennan Manning

REFLECTING

How does your response to a loved one's sexual brokenness compare with Carrie's?

EXPLORING

Like Carrie, Nehemiah knew the painful result of the past sins of his people—and the horrible reality that occurred as a result of their disobedience. He was a slave because his ancestors chose to turn their backs on God.

> "Then I acknowledged
> my sin to you and did
> not cover up my iniquity.
> I said, 'I will confess my
> transgressions to the
> LORD' and you forgave the
> guilt of my sin."
> —Psalm 32:5

Acknowledging Guilt

1. Read Nehemiah 1:5-7, 11. After Nehemiah processed his grief, what did he recall about God?

We have no record of the sins Nehemiah may have committed. To our knowledge, he was a man of faith, highly respected in the court. The fact that he had been granted a position as the cupbearer to the king underscored his unquestionable loyalty. Part of the cupbearer's role was to sip the king's drink first in case the drink was poisoned. So Nehemiah risked his life for the king on a daily basis and also served as a trusted adviser to the king.

> "He has sent me to bind
> up the brokenhearted, to
> proclaim freedom for the
> captives and release from
> darkness for the prison-
> ers, . . . to comfort all
> who mourn and provide
> for those who grieve in
> Zion—to bestow on them
> a crown of beauty instead
> of ashes, the oil of joy
> instead of mourning,
> and a garment of praise
> instead of a spirit of
> despair."
> —Isaiah 61:1-3

2. What, then, was the basis of Nehemiah's confession in verses 6 and 7?

Jesus said, "For out of the heart come evil thoughts—murder, adultery, sexual immorality, theft, false testimony, slander. These are what defile a person" (Matthew 15:19).

Nehemiah, by virtue of his humanity, knew he was capable of grievous sin. Like all of us, he had his own frailties and weaknesses. As he turned to the Lord in prayer, the magnificence of his "great and awesome God, who keeps his covenant of love with those who love him and keep his commandments" humbled his heart. He responded in reverence, with a poignant confession.

3. What weaknesses and frailties do you recognize in yourself?

4. In what ways are your sins and weaknesses similar to those of your loved one?

> "Whoever conceals their sins does not prosper, but the one who confesses and renounces them finds mercy."
> —Proverbs 28:13

Nehemiah validated his own brokenness, weakness, and powerlessness in the face of his circumstances. He did not adopt a pious façade or put on a show of false humility. He made no attempt to rationalize his sin but counted himself among the guilty, saying, "We have acted very wickedly toward you" (Nehemiah 1:7). By aligning himself with the sins of his fellow Israelites, Nehemiah acknowledged the lifelong journey that we all travel as we seek to obey God's Word and become more conformed to the image of Jesus Christ.

> "In him we have redemption through his blood, the forgiveness of sins, in accordance with the riches of God's grace that He lavished on us."
> —Ephesians 1:7-8

5. What did Nehemiah gain by acknowledging his guilt?

6. Sinful behavior patterns are often passed down from generation to generation. Our generational or family sins can impact our ability to form healthy relationships, to have positive responses to the people in our lives, and to triumph over doubt and fear. What sins have you observed in your family of origin?

7. How have these sins impacted your behavior?

> "Your [sin] is in the depths of the sea, forgiven and forgotten, and there is a little notice which says, No fishing allowed."
> —Corrie ten Boom

In our human wisdom, we usually attempt to correct what has happened to us by doing things differently in our current situation. For example, a mother who was sexually abused as a child may become overprotective in her attempt to prevent her son from experiencing the same fate. In doing so, she may unknowingly undermine his self-confidence and masculinity. Her motives are honorable, but the results are not what she expected.

> "Only reckless confidence in a Source greater than ourselves can empower us to forgive the wounds inflicted by others."
> —Brennan Manning

8. What situations have you tried to take into your own hands and change in your family, only to create new problems?

Living in the Prison of Guilt

When the news of same-sex attraction or gender confusion hits home, we tend to review every memory and agonize over every mistake. We question if we may have inadvertently contributed to our loved one's sexual brokenness. This intense introspection, coupled with our fear of other people's opinions, can forge a confining, joy-stealing prison of guilt.

9. How have you been living in a prison of guilt?

Sometimes we think that if we could pinpoint what causes a person to become a homosexual or transgendered, we could relieve our guilt. While thoroughly understanding same-sex sexual attractions or gender confusion is helpful, it may not be the answer. Once a child has made up his or her mind, the walls are already broken down and the gates have been burned, like Jerusalem's in Nehemiah's day.

In addition, we must remember there's no such thing as a perfect parent. Sometimes "good" kids come from troubled homes; and often prodigal kids come from loving, Christian homes. We can't allow the choices of our loved ones to destroy our lives.

Christian parents, especially, tend to blame themselves for the choices their mature children make—forgetting they are capable of knowing right from wrong. We cannot cause another person's homosexuality or transgenderism just as we cannot stop it.

To believe we control these things is to make ourselves martyrs and make guilt itself an idol in our lives. We must not let our desire to be a perfect parent or family member overshadow our worship of and obedience to God.

> "Who is a God like you, who pardons sin and forgives the transgression of the remnant of His inheritance? You do not stay angry forever but delight to show mercy. You will again have compassion on us; you will tread our sins underfoot and hurl all our iniquities into the depths of the sea."
> —Micah 7:18-19

Dealing with Guilt

Guilt is a state of being responsible for wrongdoing. It can also be a feeling of remorse for something we have done. Guilt usually stems from our knowledge of our own wrong thoughts or wrong actions. True guilt can be relieved by confession, repentance, a request for forgiveness, and restitution. We do not need to walk around dragging our guilt like a ball and chain.

> "Blessed are those whose dreams are shaped by their hopes and not by their hurts."
> —Dr. Robert Schuller

10. Read Nehemiah 1:8-10. What did Nehemiah do after confessing his guilt?

God's promise to the Israelites to return the exiled people to their homeland was conditional on their dependence on and obedience to Him. If we confess our own failures and humble ourselves before God, He will lift us up and be faithful to return us "home" again.

> "To walk with God in freedom, we must also walk in the bright light of holiness and truth, where God walks. . . . We cannot have fellowship with Him if we live in secret sin, pretend we are something we are not or play the game of putting on a spiritual mask (hypocrisy)."
> —Neil T. Anderson

11. List any wrong thoughts or actions you may have committed against your loved one who is struggling.

12. Take time to bring this "guilt list" to God, and pray the following prayer. Remember that forgiving ourselves can be more difficult than asking others to forgive us.

Dear heavenly Father,

Thank You for the riches of Your kindness, forbearance, and patience toward me. I bring before You the list of sins that have plagued me about my loved one's homosexuality/transgenderism. I confess that I have been guilty of the following offenses: [name your list].

I repent of my sins and ask Your forgiveness. I believe that Jesus died on the cross to forgive my sins. You said in Your Word, "If we confess our sins, He is faithful and righteous to forgive us our sins and to cleanse us from all unrighteousness" (1 John 1:9, NASB). Through this act, I accept Your pardon and will no longer carry this burden of guilt about my role in my loved one's broken sexuality. As long as this journey of dealing with my loved one's homosexuality or transgenderism lasts, I continue to claim Your grace and peace in my life.

In Jesus' name, amen.

13. Read John 16:33. What did Jesus promise His followers?

Perhaps you have had a hard time receiving God's forgiveness. Yet it is readily available to you because of Christ's sacrifice on the cross. Nothing you have done is beyond His love and mercy. His incredible gift is available for the asking. Christ's blood covers all your sins and guilt!

14. Read Psalm 103:8-12. How far does David say our sins are removed from us?

How does this knowledge comfort you?

Forgiving Our Loved Ones

Once you have received God's merciful forgiveness, complete the circle by extending forgiveness to your homosexual or transgendered loved one, if you feel ready. Forgiveness does not make an offense acceptable, but it does mean that you choose to surrender your right to be right or get even. Forgiveness does not mean forgetting either. However, refusing to forgive gives the other person permission to keep on hurting you.

15. List the offenses your loved one has committed against you.

On a separate piece of paper, write your feelings in the form of a letter you will never send. (Be sure to destroy the letter after you honestly express your feelings.)

Afterward, pray the following prayer:

Dear heavenly Father,

Thank You for the riches of Your kindness, forbearance, and patience, knowing that Your kindness has led me to repentance (Romans 2:4). I confess I have not extended that same patience and kindness toward my sexually broken loved one who has hurt me. I acknowledge the hurt and the resentment I have felt toward [name]. I confess the lack of forgiveness in my heart. Please enable me to love this person as You do.

In the name of the Lord Jesus Christ, I purpose and choose to forgive [name] for [offenses].

By this act of forgiveness, I purpose and choose to release control of the outcome of my loved one's life to You.

In Jesus' name, amen.

Nehemiah knew God loved him. Remember, you are God's beloved child; and your family member is precious to God as well. The Lord

- knows us intimately,
- listens to our every breath,
- reads our every thought,
- knows what we are going to say before we say it,
- numbers every hair on our heads,
- knew us before we were born,
- knit us together in our mothers' wombs,
- ordained all the days for us and wrote them in His book before any of them came to be,
- knows the day we will slip away from this earth to be with Him in eternity.

REBUILDING

Write a loving letter to your homosexual or transgendered family member, expressing genuine regret for any hurts you may have caused him or her. (Your list in #15 is a great place to start.) Use the word *I*, and avoid using the word *you*. Focus on letting your loved one know that you recognize the things you have done to hurt him or her and are truly sorry.

Have at least one other person read your letter—or read it to your group—and ask for feedback. The letter should reflect your humility, not judgment. When you feel confident that your letter reflects a positive attitude and tone, mail it to your loved one. God will bless your steps toward rebuilding.

If you are not yet ready to write a loving letter with sincerity, come back to this assignment when you can. Ask a friend or your group to hold you accountable to do so.

Memorize Psalm 32:5.

4

FEARING DISCLOSURE

"What is a lie?" a little girl asked her pastor. She responded, "A lie is an abomination unto the Lord." She paused thoughtfully, then added, "A very present help in time of trouble!"

As family members of homosexuals or transgendered loved ones, we often find that a lie can be "a very present help" when dealing with other people's questions regarding our loved ones.

You may relate to Susan, a mother who said, "After the initial shock of Larry's coming-out, I did everything possible to assure him of my unconditional love. We would take long walks, have long talks over coffee, or just sit together."

On the surface, Susan tried to be supportive of Larry's journey with homosexuality. But when it came to telling her family members and friends about his struggle, the words would get stuck in her throat. Even saying the word *homosexual* was difficult for her.

Invariably, friends asked about Larry. Susan didn't answer their questions directly but smiled and said, "Larry is doing fine." The most dreaded question, "Does he have a girlfriend yet?" elicited a weak smile and fake optimism. Then she replied, "He has lots of girlfriends but no one special."

When Susan and Jim's friends of twenty years called to have dinner together with them, Susan experienced renewed anxiety. She and Jim had not seen Norma and Bill since Larry had come out. What could she say when they asked about him?

She rehearsed glib answers over and over in her mind. But Norma had been her friend since childhood. While other people might not see through Susan's deceptive answers, Norma would.

Susan prayed a great deal concerning how to share the truth about Larry with her friends. As the evening progressed, Susan was able to be honest with Norma and Bill. Their gracious

"'Can anyone hide from me in a secret place? Am I not everywhere in all the heavens and earth?' says the Lord."
—Jeremiah 23:24, NLT

"If we conceal our wounds out of fear and shame, our inner darkness can neither be illuminated nor become a light for others."
—Brennan Manning

"If I hide the truth, I risk closing the doors of my openness. When I need a doctor's care, I show him my wounds."
—Pierre Wolff

"Our fear of rejection will control us to the degree by which we base our self-worth on the opinions of others rather than on our relationship with God. Our dependence on others for value brings bondage, while abiding in the truths of Christ's love and acceptance brings freedom and joy."
—Robert S. McGee

acceptance of the news encouraged Susan. They even spoke of some issues they were having with their son, Tim.

Fear of expected judgment from another person can cause us to clam up or tell a lie to avoid being hurt further. We struggle to discuss shameful issues openly, hoping the problem will go away. As a result, we carry our heavy burdens alone; and the fear and associated stress creates additional relational and physical problems.

REFLECTING

How long was it before you told anyone about your homosexual or transgendered loved one?

Who was the first person you told?

What was his or her response?

EXPLORING

Nehemiah struggled with a heavy burden too.

1. Read Nehemiah 2:1-5. How did the king know Nehemiah was struggling?

Expressing Our Grief

2. What was the king's response when Nehemiah got past his fear and told the king what was troubling him?

3. Have friends or family members noticed a difference in your face or behavior since you heard the news of your loved one's sexuality?

If so, what did they say to you?

What did you tell them?

"The ability to share our thoughts, values, and beliefs is part of *defining a self. . . . We can do it calmly, with respect for differences (others need not see things our way), and with an understanding that our way may not work for or fit others.*"
—Harriet Lerner

Our grief may be so deep we have difficulty verbalizing it to someone else. All we want to do is cry or isolate ourselves from other people in order to cope. But being willing and able to express our deepest sorrow helps us face its reality and work through it.

"The hallmark of rationalization is the intent to protect one's position rather than search for truth."
— David Tackle

4. How did you benefit from telling another person?

In ancient times, people were forbidden to be sad in the presence of a king. The king was supposed to be such a marvelous person that to be sad in front of him was an insult. If a person expressed sadness and that upset the king, he could demand, "Off with his head!"

Nehemiah displayed tremendous courage when he chose to tell the king what was going on in his heart. He knew his honesty could cost him his life.

5. What do you think gave Nehemiah the courage to speak the truth to the king?

"Be completely humble and gentle; be patient, bearing with one another in love."
—Ephesians 4:2

"Love must be sincere. Hate what is evil; cling to what is good. Be devoted to one another in love. . . . Be joyful in hope, patient in affliction, faithful in prayer."
—Romans 12:9-10, 12

Facing a Damaged Reputation

Bible scholars note that part of Nehemiah's grief may have had to do with the damaged reputation of the Jewish people. In Ezra 4:12-16, the Jewish people are indirectly referred to as wicked and rebellious. Not only was Nehemiah grieved over the sins of his people, he also worried about them falling into disrepute.

As family members, we also worry about our families falling into disrepute. A profound sense of shame accompanies the revelation of homosexuality or transgenderism even though the struggle with same-sex attraction or gender confusion is not our own. Feeling such a burden of shame can cause us to avoid others, lie, or otherwise compromise the truth out of fear and our deep sense of shame. (We will look further into this issue of shame in session 5.)

6. What has been your greatest fear about telling others of your loved one's sexual or gender issues?

7. What do you fear others will think of your family member?

8. How have you tried to protect your family member?

9. What have you worried that others would think about you?

10. How has the sexual or gender preference of your loved one affected your feelings about yourself?

Deciding to Disclose Family Secrets

Nehemiah could have chosen to keep his feelings to himself. He could have kept the king guessing about his situation, and we never would have had the miracle of a rebuilt Jerusalem.

Part of Satan's strategy against us and our hurting loved ones is to convince us it is better for everyone involved if we don't disclose our "family secrets."

11. How do the following verses impact your view of disclosure?
Galatians 6:2:

James 5:16:

The hesitation to tell anyone about our loved ones may be based on the hope they will change before anyone needs to know. Closely tied to this conviction is the fear of unnecessarily destroying our loved one's reputation.

12. What are the advantages of these arguments?

The disadvantages?

"For everything that was written in the past was written to teach us, so that through the endurance taught in the Scriptures and the encouragement they provide we might have hope."
—Romans 15:4

"Do not be anxious about anything, but in every situation by prayer and petition, with thanksgiving, present your requests to God. And the peace of God, which transcends all understanding, will guard your hearts and your minds in Christ Jesus."
—Philippians 4:6-7

13. Who benefits most in these situations?

> "But encourage one another daily, as long as it is called 'Today,' so that none of you may be hardened by sin's deceitfulness."
> —Hebrews 3:13

Often troubled children will tell only one parent about their sexual or gender confusion and request the other parent not be told. Or they may tell a sibling and ask the sibling to promise not to tell their parents for fear they would get too upset.

Keeping secrets can be devastating to a family. If a parent has not told his or her spouse, the secret is especially hard on the marriage and indicates a lack of respect for that husband or wife. It divides the family and brings additional stress into an already painful situation.

14. If you were asked to keep the secret of your family member's same-sex attraction or gender confusion from other members of your family, what did you do?

What happened as a result?

When tensions are high in parent-child relationships, gay and transgender sons or daughters may bring a third, less-threatening person into the situation to test the exposure of their secret. They may think this third party is in a position to mediate, be a peacemaker, or fix the situation. However, by inviting a third person into his or her "camp," the homosexual or transgendered family member is putting undue stress on that individual.

If you are the third person, you need to gently tell your loved one that you can no longer keep the secret. Withholding this important, yet disturbing information may create emotional distance between all parties, lead to resentment, and contribute to unhealthy relationship patterns.

You have several options for how to disclose this information. You may encourage your loved one to tell his or her parent(s) or other family members within a particular time frame. You can accompany your loved one as he or she confesses to the other parent, or you can get your loved one's consent to make the revelation in his or her presence. Or you can also volunteer to disclose confidential information through a meeting or letter, with the understanding that a family meeting with all parties will be arranged as a follow-up.

When members of the family are under the age of 18, consulting with a family counselor regarding a sibling's exposure of homosexuality or transgenderism to those children is important. Family counselors can also serve as buffers when disclosures are made.

15. Which of these choices will work best in your situation?

> "May the God of peace, who through the blood of the eternal covenant brought back from the dead our Lord Jesus, that great Shepherd of the sheep, equip you with everything good for doing His will, and may He work in us what is pleasing to him."
> —Hebrews 13:20-21

Because sexual or gender confusion is not something we struggle with personally (but is an issue for a person we love), it is important to give family members the opportunity to confess their preferences if they are adults. This does not mean you approve of their decisions. It does mean you recognize they have certain feelings and have made these decisions on their own.

Family members who cope with sexual or gender issues and are younger than eighteen need professional help. If they are living at home, getting counseling as a family will allow better understanding, interaction, and communication. Try your best to find a Christian counselor who specializes in family counseling. (You can usually obtain counseling referrals from your pastor or an ex-gay ministry near you.)

Homosexuality and gender confusion are not about sex. Deep emotional wounds have occurred that need to be healed. Referring to teens with same-sex attractions or an uncertain gender identity as "sick" may further impact their shame and solidify cultural labels. If the family is willing to go to counseling, doing so is a way of admitting help is needed for everyone. After family counseling, specialists in sexual issues can be contacted and individual counseling pursued.

16. What problems have you encountered in sharing with others about your loved one?

In observing Nehemiah's actions, we find a model for how to disclose our own hurts and anguish to others. We can examine Nehemiah's actions and follow the same steps he took in approaching a difficult issue.

(1) Nehemiah spent many hours in prayer (Nehemiah 1:4). His courage to speak truth was made possible with God's help, and seeking God's direction in prayer gave him strength. (See Acts 4:13.)

There is no substitute for prayer in our lives. In prayer, we open our hearts and lives to the only One who can change us and offer us peace. Through prayer, the Holy Spirit guides us, revealing to whom we should confide and also giving us the words we should speak.

(2) Nehemiah knew the king was in a position to help him and was able to talk with him because they had a trusted relationship. As the king's cupbearer, Nehemiah had shown himself valuable and faithful. His good reputation helped when it came time for him to request a favor.

(3) When the king asked what was wrong, Nehemiah shot up a quick, fervent prayer and responded with the truth (Nehemiah 2:4). The Holy Spirit helps us know how to present the truth (John 16:13). By sharing our burdens with other people, we fulfill the biblical mandate to "carry each other's burdens, and . . . you will fulfill the law of Christ" (Galatians 6:2). Even if we cannot be entirely open, we can ask for prayers for our family members.

(4) Nehemiah spoke the truth about himself. He did not blame his Jewish relatives for the destruction in Jerusalem. He described the problem in the city as he saw it. Likewise, it's important for us to speak the truth about our problem without placing blame or judgment.

Finding Help for Yourself

As a family member of a person dealing with such a difficult issue, you must look for spiritual encouragement and prayer support for yourself, as well. You don't have to carry this burden of grief alone! Find a trusted Christian friend, mentor, counselor, or pastor to encourage you and help you through this painful time.

17. Who do you think you can go to for encouragement and prayer support?

REBUILDING

On a sheet of unlined paper, draw a large circle representing your family of origin. Inside that circle, draw several smaller circles representing your parents, siblings, and yourself, using first names or initials for each person.

On the outside of the large circle, draw smaller circles for family friends. Now draw a solid line from your circle to the circles of family members and friends to whom you feel close. If the relationship with family members or friends is not close, draw a dotted line between the circles.

For example, if you have a twin sister you are close to but you do not have a close relationship with your father, you would draw a solid line between your circle and your twin sister's circle and a dotted line between your circle and your father's circle.

If you have been able to share the news of homosexuality or transgenderism in your family with some of your family members or friends, color in the circles of those people. Compare and contrast the reasons why you were able to tell some family members but not others.

Share your diagram with a trusted friend or your small group. Explain why the relationships are the way you drew them. What is significant about each relationship? What might you do to make it easier to tell family members who don't yet know? Whom might you consider disclosing to next?

As a second exercise, draw another circle to represent your immediate family. Within the larger circle, draw smaller circles to represent your spouse and children. Draw the lines indicating the relationships with each one. Compare and contrast these circles with the ones from your family of origin.

How do you think both families' interactions have affected your willingness to share about your homosexual or transgender loved one?

Memorize Hebrews 3:13.

5

CONFRONTING SHAME

Oh hallelujah, Denise thought, as her mother told her she was looking for a way to escape from Dad. *God is about to answer my prayers—finally!*

A glorious relief washed over Denise. *Maybe we could be a real family now! Maybe I could even have some friends over!* She pictured life at Grandma's house, spending evenings playing with her sister and brothers. She was thrilled at the prospect.

No more of Dad's bizarre behavior—no more would he be chasing her around the yard, falling on her, and acting inappropriately. It was all she could hope for.

Since third grade, life had never been the same. Her Mom began working the second and third shifts in a nursing home, leaving Denise in charge of her younger brothers and sister.

Denise hated the fact that her mother worked. She blamed her father because he regularly put them into bad financial situations. She never knew where the money went; she only knew there was never enough.

Shame washed over Denise as she remembered when she first learned her Daddy's secret. She was nine years old, cleaning up the kitchen when her father leaned on the counter and said, "Denise, come outside with me. I want to talk with you." Denise dreaded to know what her father had to say. He was always so angry. *What did he want this time?*

She followed him out the back door and along the dirt path to a small hill behind the house. They both sat down; and her father began, "I want to be a woman." He continued with a faraway look in his eyes, "You know how you can tell when I'm feeling especially feminine? It's when I sit with my legs crossed, you know, like your dance classes. . . . I wish I could wear a

> "Shame affects all of us to one degree or another. . . . Most of us experience the uncomfortable, sometimes excruciating symptoms of shame, but we've had them so long, we think they're normal."
> —Marie Powers

> "I sought the Lord, and He answered me; he delivered me from all my fears. Those who look to him are radiant; their faces are never covered with shame."
> —Psalm 34:4-5

> "When you were slaves to sin, you were free from the control of righteousness. What benefit did you reap at that time from the things you are now ashamed of? Those things result in death! But now that you have been set free from sin and have become slaves of God, the benefit you reap leads to holiness, and the result is eternal life."
>
> —Romans 6:20-22

> "It used to be that I never felt safe with myself unless I was performing flawlessly. My desire to be perfect had transcended my desire for God."
>
> —Brennan Manning

dress. . . . I wish I could twirl a baton. You understand, don't you, Denise?"

Understand that my dad wants to wear dresses? Understand that while he was taking me to the store to buy my training bras, he wanted to try them on himself? How could I understand? I was shocked and appalled. . . . I just lost my dad.

Denise came back to reality. Now there was hope! Let her dad pursue his strange desires. *Maybe life could be different if we got away from him.*

But eventually her shoulders drooped again. Denise's mother let the matter drop. Her chronically angry husband had told his nine-year-old daughter intimate details about his sex life, had confided his desire to become a woman, and had sexually molested her. But when it was time for action, Mom once again buried her head in the sand and pretended everything was fine.

REFLECTING
How does your shame compare to that of Denise and her mother?

EXPLORING
Nehemiah and the Israelites encountered shame too.

1. Reread Nehemiah 1:4-7; 2:17; and 4:1-3. In Nehemiah 4, Sanballet and Tobiah attempted to stop the rebuilding of the wall by shaming the Israelites. What kind of shame did the Israelites experience?

2. What did Sanballet and Tobiah say and do to shame the Israelites?

3. In what ways do people in our culture shame parents and families who have sexually broken loved ones?

The Problem of Shame

Shame is a normal aspect of human experience but is rarely defined or openly discussed. People respond differently to shame, based on their personalities and circumstances; but acknowledging shame appears to be shameful in and of itself.

Shame is the subjective, painful humiliation or distress that accompanies wrongful behavior, feelings of unworthiness, or embarrassment. Guilt is the fact or state of having committed a specific wrong or offense. Guilt addresses the act; shame condemns the guilty person. We feel guilty for what we have done; we feel shame for who we are.

For example, when a family member "comes out," we experience a sense of guilt for not being a better parent, spouse, or sibling. Memories of past sins or mistakes haunt us. Guilt acknowledges those slipups and regrets having made them. Shame piggybacks on the guilt, condemning who we are and adding painful judgments to the mental accusations.

Instead of acknowledging our loved ones' individual sovereignty to live their lives and make their own decisions, we blame ourselves. Along with the stress of our shame, we perceive a loss of respect from people we once trusted: friends and neighbors, family members, pastors, and other Christians.

The fear of shame and exposure to social disgrace can lead us to hide from other people, deny what has happened, or deceive others in an attempt to protect ourselves or our loved one.

Biblical Perspective of Shame

4. Shame began with Adam and Eve. Read Genesis 2:15-17, 25; 3:6-7. What was God's first command to them?

5. How is shame related to obedience?

> "Perfectionism is a self-destructive and addictive belief system that fuels this primary thought: 'If I look perfect, live perfectly, and do everything perfectly, I can avoid or minimize the painful feelings of shame, judgment, and blame.'"
> —Brené Brown

> "But those who trust in idols, who say to images, 'You are our gods,' will be turned back in utter shame."
> —Isaiah 42:17

"I not only have my secrets, I am my secrets. And you are your secrets. Our secrets are human secrets, and our trusting each other enough to share them with each other has much to do with the secret of what it is to be human."
—Frederick Buechner

When we disobey God, our feelings of shame surface as we deal with our wrongful actions. We have fallen short of God's standards, and our wrongdoing has caused a breach in our relationship with Him. God uses shame to bring us back to Him. The Holy Spirit convicts us and prompts us to confess our sin and seek His forgiveness and restoration. Genuine brokenness brought about by shame leads us to bow before God in genuine humility with an attitude of penitent confession, not in defensiveness or pride.

6. Toward the end of his life, King David disobeyed God by counting his troops instead of trusting his Lord. In 2 Samuel 24:10, we see him awakening to his guilt and shame. What was David's response?

"Because the Sovereign Lord helps me, I will not be disgraced. Therefore have I set my face like flint, and I know I will not be put to shame."
—Isaiah 50:7

When the reality of our sin is exposed like David's was, our response should be acknowledging the truth of what the Holy Spirit has shown us. True repentance brings a heart broken over our sin and rebellion toward God. Failure in the eyes of other people is not nearly as important as admitting that we have broken God's law and then repenting of what we have done. Shame brings about a heart of true repentance.

Subjective Shame

One kind of shame is subjective shame. It is not necessarily attached to wrongdoing, although it may be attached to the unfinished business of confession and repentance from a sinful act. More often, it is ascribed as low self-image, a sense of falling short as a human being, worthlessness, or feeling defective and undesirable.

The deepest beliefs about ourselves are born of life experiences. These experiences lead us to believe something is flawed and inherently wrong with us. We are too sinful, bad, or defective for God to love or forgive us. A loving, forgiving, grace-giving God is foreign to a person filled with subjective shame. To live in subjective shame is to live a life of constant defeat. We feel useless and powerless in ourselves. As we turn our lives over to God and learn to live our lives in Him, in His strength, we become strong and victorious.

One of our most basic needs as human beings is the need to belong, to feel loved and accepted as we are. When we are driven by a fear of rejection or abandonment, we trust our sense of value to people instead of God. We rely on others to find us acceptable and give them the right to judge us—a prerogative that should be God's alone. In doing so, we create a false self, an impostor who hides the authentic self and relies on achievement and performance.

> "Instead of your shame, you will receive a double portion, and instead of disgrace you will rejoice in your inheritance. And so you will inherit a double portion in your land, and everlasting joy will be yours."
> —Isaiah 61:7

Undeserved Shame

Shame also takes up residence in our hearts through emotions, words, and actions of other people. Name-calling; excessive teasing; bullying; slander; belittling; physical, emotional, spiritual, or sexual abuse; mockery; comparison to others; emotional enmeshment; addictive behaviors; inappropriate sexual behavior or remarks; physical or emotional neglect; negatively emphasizing racial or physical differences that cannot be changed; and deliberately ignoring a person can bring about a sense of low self-esteem and worthlessness—falling short as a human being.

Our interpretations or beliefs about ourselves are heavily influenced by how others see us. If I believe people generally see me as worthless and don't respect or care about my well-being, I will tend to collect data that proves my assumptions about myself are correct.

Children do not know how to make sense of their experiences or evaluate adult behavior, so they incorrectly believe these behaviors and events reflect on them. This undeserved shame buries itself deep in the subconscious and has a powerful effect on relationships as they grow up.

7. Describe one instance of undeserved shame from your life.

8. Describe one instance of undeserved shame from the life of your homosexual or transgendered family member.

51

> "We cannot grow when we are in shame, and we can't use shame to change ourselves or others."
>
> —Brené Brown

9. A biblical example of someone who experienced undeserved shame is Hannah. Read 1 Samuel 1:6-7, 10-11, and 19-20. What was the undeserved shame?

10. What was Hannah's response to this shame?

11. What did God do for Hannah as a result of her response?

Hannah prayed and said, "'My heart rejoices in the LORD; in the LORD my horn is lifted high'" (1 Samuel 2:1). To have one's horn lifted up by God is to be delivered from disgrace to a place of honor and strength. Hannah's shame was taken away!

Coping with Shame

Shame becomes a prison, encasing us behind iron bars of bondage that need to be broken. God knows about our shame, and He wants to turn it into freedom.

If you have tried to run your life and have disobeyed God, take time to confess your bondage, the hurts and mistakes of your past. "Grieve, mourn and wail" (James 4:9) over your sins and the sins committed against you. Acknowledge your hopelessness and powerlessness to change yourself and your loved one. Visualize handing your shame to Jesus and feeling Him embrace you as He wraps you in His robe of righteousness. If you are a child of the King of Kings, the Lord of Lords, you're a new creature in Christ. God has called you out of darkness into His wonderful light, and He wants to transform you into His image.

Transformation takes time and deliberate steps. Choose to bathe yourself in God's Word daily. Confess to Him the lies you have believed about yourself, and ask the Holy Spirit to show you the truth of who you are in Christ. Don't give up. God rewards people who earnestly seek Him. One day you will not even remember the cloak of shame you wore. You will persevere because you have been transformed by God who has been formed in you.

Jesus and Shame

Jesus understands shame (Hebrews 12:2-3). He was condemned to die on a cross, a punishment consigned to the worst criminals of His day. They beat Him, spit in His face, and struck Him with their fists. They whipped Him; placed a crown of thorns on His head; and mocked Him by saying, "Hail, king of the Jews!" (Matthew 27:29). Jesus endured the most severe physical and emotional suffering a human being could endure, and the form of His death is regarded as the most shameful.

> "The enemy works overtime to keep us in shame. He knows if he can keep us in shame, he can minimize our intimacy with God."
> —Mike Bickle

Yet Hebrews 12:2 tells us that Jesus "for the joy set before him . . . endured the cross, scorning its shame." Jesus' joy was the pleasure of reversing the tragic fall of man that occurred in the Garden of Eden. The joy of knowing Satan's purpose for destroying man was blocked; and through His death, Jesus would bring "many sons and daughters to glory" (Hebrews 2:10). His imminent joy would remove the sting of His present suffering.

Jesus' shame never became subjective for Him. He was able to scorn, or despise, the shame because He saw it for what it was: Satan's attempt to stop Him from doing God's will.

12. How willing are you to despise the shame you are enduring from sexual brokenness in your family in order to fulfill God's will for your life?

REBUILDING

Turn an unlined sheet of paper horizontally, and draw four columns on it. At the top of each column, from left to right, write the following titles: *The Shame I Carry*, *The Roots of My Shame*, *The Person I Need to Forgive*, and *God's Truth for Me*.

Think of one memory of shame you have carried since childhood, and write it in the first column. As you contemplate this situation, think of the circumstances that may have created it; and write these in the second column. If someone deliberately shamed or harmed you, write his or her name in the third column. Then express your feelings about that person to God, and ask Him to help you forgive him or her. Finally, find a Bible verse that contradicts what you have believed about yourself as a result of your shame, and write it out in the last column.

Do the same for other shameful situations if you so desire.

If you feel comfortable doing so, share your memory with a trusted friend, family member, or your small group.

Memorize Psalm 34:4-5.

INSPECTING THE BROKENNESS

Lauren was 22, a *summa cum laude* graduate of a Christian college, living at home until she could get on her feet. She had been a lovely, sweet, affectionate girl and as feminine as could be—two years ago. Now she seemed sullen and noncommunicative. Her femininity seemed to vanish. She was hanging around with a new crowd, staying out late, and separating herself from her family. When her parents, Tom and Ellen, tried to talk with Lauren, she alternated between fits of anger and weeping, which made communication difficult.

Accidentally one day, Ellen found an email addressed to Lauren and read it. "Oh, my goodness!" Ellen exclaimed, her eyes filling with tears. "What is this?"

As she continued reading, she became more and more upset. The letter had romantic undertones, leaving Ellen immobilized and shaken. It was clearly more than a friendly note.

In tears, she called Tom at work and insisted he come home right away. Together they pored over the email in shock and dismay. Their conversation continued well into the night.

When they confronted Lauren the next day, Tom and Ellen found out she was communicating with a lesbian lover on the Internet. Their first reaction was shock and disbelief. Surely their beautiful daughter could not be involved with another woman!

Wisely, Tom and Ellen sought help for themselves first, then asked Lauren if she would be willing to see a counselor.

After a period of time, Lauren met with a counselor and finally opened up. "I've felt this way all my life," she said, "ever

> "Starting with the rather too pretty young woman, say, and the charming but rather unstable young man who together know no more about being parents than they do about the far side of the moon, the world sets in to making us into what the world would like us to be, and because we have to survive after all, we try to make ourselves into something that we hope the world will like better than it apparently did the selves we originally were.
>
> That is the story of all of our lives, needless to say, and in the process of living out that story, the original, shimmering self gets buried so deep that most of us end up hardly living out of it at all. Instead, we live out all the other selves which we are constantly putting on and off like coats and hats against the world's weather."
>
> —Frederick Buechner

"I had a very close relationship with my mother and a somewhat distant one with my father. . . . In my adolescence, I warred with my father and sided in [sic] my mother in the family fights . . . and in all of this, I suppose, I followed a typical pattern of homosexual development."
—Andrew Sullivan, gay activist

since I can remember. I just never have been able to talk with Mom and Dad about it."

Over several sessions, she painfully brought to light those things that bothered her deeply. "I feel anger and resentment toward men, all of whom I feel will use me. I was molested by a male cousin at the age of 13. My mother was sexually abused by her father as a child and had several affairs while I was growing up. She attempted to make me strong and independent, so I wouldn't need men.

"My father despised her tears and made me feel it wasn't okay to be a girl. So I felt contempt for my mother's weaknesses and therefore hated that I was a woman."

When Tom and Ellen met with Lauren's counselor, they had no idea of the hurt that had come to their daughter—or how their own issues had impacted her. Lauren's revelation of same-sex attractions opened up a lot of pain in the family, and her journey to wholeness became a healing journey for Tom and Ellen as well.

REFLECTING

On a scale of 1 to 10, with 10 being hardest, how difficult has it been for you to look at the brokenness in yourself and your family of origin?

EXPLORING

Nehemiah, too, went through the process of looking at brokenness in preparation for rebuilding. Although his situation involved the physical walls of a city, we can learn principles from his experience that apply to our families.

1. Read Nehemiah 2:6-16. Why did the king give Nehemiah permission to go to Jerusalem?

Inspecting the Brokenness

2. What did Nehemiah do when he arrived in Jerusalem?

3. How do you think he felt when seeing the broken walls and gates of his beloved city?

"Dear friends, do not be surprised at the fiery ordeal that has come on you to test you, as though something strange were happening to you. But rejoice inasmuch as you participate in the sufferings of Christ, so that you may be overjoyed when his glory is revealed."
—1 Peter 4:12-13

While Nehemiah was a Jewish slave under Persian rule, he also had been living in the king's court. He could have chosen to ignore the plight of his people. After all, he was well taken care of, living among wealthy people and enjoying the benefits of the Persian court. How difficult it must have been for him to finally face the devastation of his beloved, ancestral home. Nehemiah showed incredible courage to return to a place that represented so much pain to him and his forefathers.

4. When we consider how difficult it is for us to face our demons, we can begin to comprehend the pain our homosexual or transgendered loved ones are in. What is the most painful issue you've learned about in your family?

Unearthing Memories

Picking his way through the devastation, Nehemiah must have had flashbacks, mental pictures of the genteel way of his Jewish ancestors that no longer existed. All he could see now was the burned rubble, evidence of the enemy invasion that destroyed homes, left families divided, and removed the brightest and most talented among them as hostages. How his heart must have ached!

Like Nehemiah, we are flooded with memories of what used to be. We long for the days before homosexuality or transgenderism and wish we had never encountered all the problems that have surfaced: conflict among family members, unending questions, guilt trips, deception, and most of all the pain it has brought to everyone involved.

5. What painful memories surface when you think about your present situation with your loved one?

6. What is one good memory you can hang on to?

> "Arise, cry out in the night as the watches of the night begin; pour out your heart like water in the presence of the Lord. Lift up your hands to him for the lives of your children."
> —Lamentations 2:19

Dealing with homosexuality or transgenderism takes tremendous courage. It means facing family secrets we believed had long been buried or dealt with. Those moments of trauma return to us, dressed in the clothing of shame and blame, painful to remember and troubling to acknowledge. Sometimes we would rather be dead than deal with the impact those events have had on our loved ones.

When moments of trauma are relived, it is tempting to shame or blame other family members. We become defensive and say things we wish we hadn't.

> "God does not call His people to triumph before He has exercised them in the warfare of suffering."
> —John Calvin

7. What is one thing you said to a family member that you wish you had never said?

8. What can you do to repair the damage that resulted from those words?

Nehemiah chose to examine the gates and walls at night. Darkness not only gave him a chance to express his emotions unobserved, but it also allowed him to take his time viewing the destruction without interference from other people. He was not yet ready to talk about what God had put in his heart to do. Observing the destruction at night allowed him to put together a plan for restoration before he was saddled with questions by opinionated onlookers.

Like Nehemiah, the night becomes a time when we can express our emotions unabashedly but also listen to the still, small voice of God telling us what He wants us to do.

9. How are the nights more difficult for you?

"The heart is deceitful above all things and beyond cure. Who can understand it?"
—Jeremiah 17:9

10. What word of hope has God given you to cling to as you confront the reality of your situation? (If you don't have a word of hope, ask God to give you one.)

"Our Christian growth is a battle against Satan in our own hearts. This front, for most of us, is the hardest. It's not easy to fight evil in another person. . . . But it's grueling to face the dark, cold reality that we have to battle against our own vicious and destructive thoughts, emotions, and actions."
—Dan Allender

Assessing Emotional and Spiritual Damage

Assessing emotional and spiritual damage to our family members is much more difficult than assessing the physical damage Nehemiah had to face. Physical damage can be seen. Emotional and spiritual damage is hidden, not only from the family but often from the family member who has confessed same-sex attractions or gender confusion. Recovery will take time, prayer, and lots of communication.

11. What clues or suspicions did you have about your loved one's sexual or gender issues before he or she made it known?

What did you do in response to this information?

12. What regrets, if any, do you have about how you handled this information?

"Denial destroys a person's relationships, resulting in spiritual sterility in relationship with God, loss of authenticity in relationship to oneself, and absence of intimacy in relationships with others."
—Nancy Groom

The destruction of Jerusalem came through an enemy invasion by the Babylonians. Even though the Israelites were God's chosen people, they suffered severely at the hands of their enemies.

As Christians, we often think we should not be subject to the same pain or hardship that unbelievers experience. It's as if God owes us protection since we have been faithful believers or church attendees. We also have been misled by Bible teachers who teach that health, wealth, and happiness are signs of God's divine blessing.

13. How do you reconcile being a Christian and experiencing pain in your life?

"'Come, let us return to the LORD. He has torn us to pieces; now he will heal us. He has injured us; now he will bandage our wounds. In just a short time he will restore us, so that we may live in his presence. Oh, that we might know the LORD! Let us press on to know him. He will respond to us as surely as the arrival of dawn or the coming of rains in early spring.'"
—Hosea 6:1-3, NASB

14. How has the impact of your homosexual or transgendered loved one affected your faith?

Questioning God

"'For my thoughts are not your thoughts, neither are your ways my ways,' declares the LORD" (Isaiah 55:8). He is not the author of evil, but also we do not know His ultimate goal for us or our loved ones. Sometimes tragedy occurs in order to make us more like Christ. Other times, God is testing us, pushing us to new growth and maturity.

Often we are unaware of the areas in our lives that God wants to change. Perhaps there is unforgiveness, unconfessed sin, or idolatry (worship of self, others, or created things instead of God) in our hearts. Time with God will help us face these areas of needed growth.

Moses touched on this concept in Deuteronomy 8:2: "Remember how the LORD your God led you all the way in the wilderness these forty years, to humble and test you in order to know what was in your heart, whether or not you would keep his commands."

It is tempting to be self-righteous before our loved ones come out of the closet. It is easy to label our sexually confused loved one as the villain and ourselves as righteous and good. But God sees our hearts; and we, too, desperately need His mercy and grace.

The heart is the seat of our mind, will, and emotions. While we may have asked Jesus into our hearts to forgive us of our sins a long time ago, we have not arrived spiritually. (Nor has anyone else.) He is still in the process of making our minds, wills, and emotions holy. He is asking us to yield completely to Him, to His will and way in our hearts.

15. In what ways does the pride in your own heart show up?

16. What behaviors have you been quick to judge in other people?

Which of these behaviors do you see in yourself?

"It makes a tremendous difference in our lives when we trust that the same God who wounds also heals."
—John Calvin

"When chaos breaks loose—in world events, in relationships, in work, in health matters—my weakness is all too obvious. I realize how much I need someone whose power is far greater than mine will ever be."
—Jan Winebrenner

Examining Our Brokenness

The greatest damage to any individual or family is the impact sin has on our relationship with God and with one another. A basic need in this life is for relationship. If we are to face life as it really is and make the inner changes that genuinely will transform our lives, we will have to take a fresh look at ourselves and step out of denial.

We cannot change another person, but God can change us if we will allow Him to do so. As we begin to change, the relationship with our loved ones changes. Our family members are perceptive and know our weaknesses. We cannot preach to them without looking at our own issues. (See *Boundaries: When to Say Yes, How to Say No to Take Control of Your Life* by Henry Cloud and John Townsend.)

If we can sincerely humble ourselves before God and our loved ones, acknowledge we have made mistakes or had sin in our own lives, and ask for forgiveness, God can use our brokenness to bring healing in us—and in them. By being humble, real, and vulnerable, we affirm that knowing Jesus makes a difference.

At the same time, every relationship is two-sided. We are not totally responsible for our loved ones' choices. Knowing what I should take responsibility for versus what they should take responsibility for brings freedom. By being open about our part of the problem, we help our loved ones own their parts. Reconciliation does not happen easily because both parties are often blind to their own issues. It may take years to work out all the disagreements in a relationship. What is important is to keep listening to God's voice and be willing to make the changes He reveals to us.

17. What have you preached about to your loved one in the past?

> "If we lean on God, trusting that His promises are true and that He will direct us each day, we can begin to experience the peace that we long to have in the midst of this traumatic family situation."
> —Anita Worthen

> "'I will refine them like silver and test them like gold. They will call on my name and I will answer them; I will say, 'They are my people,' and they will say, 'the LORD is our God.'"
> —Zechariah 13:9

18. How is God changing you in relation to this issue?

> "The greatest among you will be your servant. For those who exalt themselves will be humbled, and those who humble themselves will be exalted."
> —Matthew 23:11-12

Trusting God

Learning about homosexuality or transgenderism in our families helps us understand how little control we have over what happens to us or our family members. We try to do everything we can to love, protect, and bring them up in the nurture and admonition of the Lord. But we are not in control. God is. And He graciously gives all of us free will to make our own decisions.

The sexual confusion of your loved one is not a surprise to God. It is His desire to bring healing and wholeness to the entire family. Homosexuality and transgenderism are often symptoms of deeper sin issues in our hearts and homes. They are cries for help from our family members, an indication that all is not well in our "peaceful" situation.

God desires to bring health to His children and our family members. But we must be willing to acknowledge that there is something in us that needs to change and heal. Are you willing to release your control into the hands of God who knows best what needs to happen in your life and the life of your family member?

The following prayer by A. W. Tozer, a pastor and prolific author, may help you understand how to release control to God:

Lord, I would trust You completely; I would be altogether Yours; I would exalt You above all. I desire that I may feel no sense of possessing anything outside of You. I want constantly to be aware of Your overshadowing Presence and to hear Your speaking Voice. I long to live in restful sincerity of heart. I want to live so fully in the Spirit that all my thought may be as sweet incense ascending to You and every act of my life may be an act of worship. Therefore I pray in the words of Your great servant of old, "I beseech You so for to cleanse the intent of mine heart with the unspeakable gift of Your grace, that I may perfectly love You and worthily praise You." And all this I confidently believe You wilt grant me through the merits of Jesus Christ Your Son. Amen (The Pursuit of God, Camp Hill, PA: Christian Publications, n.d., p. 128, pronouns updated).

REBUILDING

Reflect on the areas of your life that may have had a negative impact on your sexually confused loved one. Jot them below, and allow a few days for God to speak to you about them. Then talk over your thoughts with a counselor or someone who knows you well.

After you have thought and prayed, make an appointment with your loved one. Choose a private place that will allow you to talk together easily. If you are a parent, meet with your son or daughter alone, not with your spouse.

With an attitude of humility, let your loved one know you have come to share some things that may have had a detrimental impact on your relationship. Talk only about what *you* have done that is negative. Do not talk about your spouse's or anyone else's role. This conversation is only about you and what you may have done. Allow your spouse to speak for him or herself when they meet privately. If you are a parent and the discussion turns to your spouse, say, "We are not here to talk about _____; he or she will be talking with you separately."

When you have finished, ask your loved one if he or she has anything to say to you. Silence can be deafening, but wait until he or she speaks. Then, listen, listen, listen. Ask for further clarification if necessary. Wait until he or she has finished, then ask if you may respond. Apologize where needed and receive what has been said without defending yourself, hard as that may be. When your conversation is over, affirm your love for him or her and your desire to remain in relationship. Let your loved one know you are always open and willing to talk again, if he or she desires to do so.

Encounters like this one with your loved ones may or may not make a difference in their pursuit of same-sex relationships or a gender change. However, you are building a relationship with them and laying the groundwork for further healing.

Memorize Hosea 6:1-3.

7

PREPARING TO REBUILD

"I need to tell you what I'm feeling, but it's not pretty," Jack confessed to our support group with deep anguish in his voice. He leaned forward in his chair, hands clasped tightly together.

"I'm so angry at God right now!" he exclaimed. "You know I teach, and I know how important it is to give immediate feedback; but God isn't giving me anything. I pray for my daughter every day, and nothing changes. I'm ready to give up my faith. What good does it do?"

This father's only child, a beautiful daughter, had been raised in Christian schools and trained to be in ministry, yet was now living in a committed gay relationship. We can imagine this father's pain. He had made a huge investment in his daughter's life, only to see those dreams die. The grief was overwhelming.

> "'I have loved you with an everlasting love; I have drawn you with unfailing kindness. I will build you up again.'"
> —Jeremiah 31:3

> "They will rebuild the ancient ruins and restore the places long devastated."
> —Isaiah 61:4

REFLECTING

What do you think was the most difficult aspect of Jack's journey with his daughter?

When have you, like Jack, been ready to give up your faith because of the homosexuality or gender confusion of your loved one?

65

"Dear friends, do not be surprised at the fiery ordeal that has come on you to test you, as though something strange were happening to you. But rejoice inasmuch as you participate in the sufferings of Christ, so that you may be overjoyed when his glory is revealed."
—1 Peter 4:12-13

EXPLORING

Nehemiah, too, faced a great disappointment after surveying the broken walls and gates of Jerusalem.

1. Read Nehemiah 2:17-18. What was Nehemiah's attitude after his survey?

What did he do?

Rebuilding the wall was an important part of God's plan for the Jewish people. Without walls, Jerusalem was completely open and vulnerable to its enemies. Because the Jews alone were God's people, the broken walls were an affront to God's character and reputation, as well as a blight on the Jewish people.

A mature man of God, Nehemiah knew the devastation was overwhelming; and he could not do the work of rebuilding alone. He refused to let the terrible rubble—the broken and burned walls—and Sanballat and Tobiah's mocking and ridicule discourage him. He owned the problem and asked for the people's partnership. He didn't beg, manipulate, or make deals. He relied on "the gracious hand of . . . God upon [him] and what the king had said to [him]" (v. 18). His words were enough to create an inward motivation in the hearts of the people who would assist him in rebuilding.

2. How much do you wish to rebuild your family?

3. How does your attitude about rebuilding compare to Nehemiah's?

Why?

Living with "Broken Walls"

With the news of homosexuality or transgenderism in our families, anger, grief, shame, guilt, and hopelessness all become part of our journey. Our self-worth has been destroyed. Our faith is on trial. Nothing we knew or valued is the same anymore. The strength and joy with which we lived our Christian lives has been temporarily dismantled. We wonder if God is still interested in us. Where has He been in our tragedy? What happened to His promises we relied on?

"In His great love, God leads us through experiences that are difficult but essential to our growth and development."
—Robert McGee

We are beaten down and immobilized by the enemy's attack. Furthermore, Satan has silenced us. Perhaps we have been leaders ourselves, but now we feel such a sense of shame and failure we no longer feel worthy to minister to others.

4. What impact has your family situation had on your Christian testimony?

Changing Our Focus

Struggles with our faith tend to come when we observe our loved ones and don't seem to see any changes in them. We begin to question God. "If God hasn't answered my prayers, maybe He is okay with my son/daughter/spouse/brother/sister/friend's sexual brokenness."

Ultimately, the healing of homosexual or transgender persons begins with our loved ones' decision to want help. The Holy Spirit is ready and willing to draw their hearts to God, and it is good to pray for our loved ones in this way. God would not have us be victims or continue to focus on self-pity. The longer we spend feeling sorry for ourselves, the more we will be defeated by the enemy of our souls. We cannot control our adult family members or change them. Only God can bring about the changes that are needed for them to live holy lives.

Like Nehemiah, we must choose to believe God will provide the strength for us to carry on. To deny God's power to work in the lives of our loved ones is an affront to God's character and an admission of our lack of faith. When we have given our lives to Christ, His resurrection power is within us. Nothing is impossible with His help.

"'In repentance and rest is your salvation, in quietness and trust is your strength.'"
—Isaiah 30:15

5. What aspect of your journey do you most need to turn over to God?

6. Select a verse (or verses) you can cling to for seeing God's miracle in the life of your loved one, and memorize it. Here are a few you may wish to choose from: Matthew 19:26; Mark 10:27; Luke 18:27; Hebrews 11:6; and Jeremiah 31:16-17.

Understanding Suffering

Suffering is one way God brings about changes in us, as well as our loved ones. No one wants to hurt, but we learn important lessons through suffering. When a child sticks his finger in a socket and receives an electric shock, he no longer disobeys Mom and Dad. Touching a hot stove results in the same lesson. Until the prodigal son was starving in a pig's pen, he had no desire to go home to his father.

Jesus had to suffer and die, so our sins would be forgiven. Two verses in Hebrews 5 highlight this truth: "During the days of Jesus' life on earth, he offered up prayers and petitions with loud cries and tears to the one who could save him from death, and he was heard because of his reverent submission. Although He was a Son, he learned obedience from what he suffered" (vv. 7-8, NIV84).

Jesus' prayers were heard, but God's ultimate plan for His life took precedence over saving Jesus from the cross. And Jesus submitted to God's plan, even when it meant a great deal of pain and anguish for Him. How blessed we are that Jesus was willing to pay the price for each of our sins.

7. What good changes has suffering made in your life since you began this study?

Grieving is diminished when we take our eyes off our broken dreams and implement a plan to rebuild. The emotions that accompany grief can be rechanneled into creative energy needed to construct new walls.

Surrendering Our Loved Ones

On our journey with sexual brokenness, we will not find peace until we have totally turned our loved ones over to God. Letting go of a beloved family member and giving him or her back to God is not easy—and feels like losing control. Because we are. We surrender to God all our efforts to convince that person to change, to bargain or bribe them to accommodate our wishes. We give back our role as God to God Himself. We cannot change our loved ones. Only God can. Changing ourselves is difficult enough. Thomas à Kempis said it aptly: "Be not angry that you cannot make others as you wish them to be, since you cannot make yourself as you wish to be."

The following descriptions may help you in your effort to let go:

> "We have to recognize that sin is a fact of life, not just a shortcoming. Sin is blatant mutiny against God, and either sin or God must die in my life. . . . We must mentally bring ourselves to terms with this fact of sin. It is the only explanation why Jesus Christ came to earth, and it is the explanation of the grief and sorrow of life."
> —Oswald Chambers

To Let Go

- To let go is to realize I am no longer in control of your life.
- To let go is to grieve the inability to control your thoughts and actions.
- To let go is to sacrifice any attempt to control you, but to give you over to God.
- To let go is to realize you are an adult, and I no longer need to make decisions for you.
- To let go is to give godly wisdom and advice when requested and understand the ultimate decision to take or leave the advice is yours.
- To let go is to watch you make your own decisions and let you reap the consequences of those decisions without rescuing you.
- To let go is to see you live your life as you wish without stopping you.
- To let go is to mourn our change of roles in each other's life.
- To let go is to realize I cannot change you, only God can.
- To let go is to find my life in God—apart from you.

8. Which of the above statements is the most difficult one to give up?

Why?

"Though no one can go back and make a brand-new start, anyone can start from now and make a brand-new ending."
—Carl Bard

Letting go is one of the most difficult decisions you can make, but one of the most important steps in the relationship with your loved one. Barbara Johnson, author of *Where Does a Mother Go to Resign?*, tells the story of being so desperate about her son that she almost committed suicide. Through this experience, she finally let go of her gay son and gave him back to God.

9. How is God showing you to let go of your loved one?

Moving Forward

Once you have surrendered your loved one to God, it is time to see what He would have you do to strengthen yourself and your family. Rebuilding is about healing relationships with God and with others. Experts who have studied troubled kids identify the dynamics listed in question #10 below as occurring often in hurting families. These peculiarities in and of themselves do not create dysfunctional families but may be factors. They often are related to our own sins or the impact of others' sins on our lives, sometimes referred to as "generational sin."

Sin is the manifestation of our self-life. Two of the words used for sin in the New Testament are: (1) *Hamartia*, a shooting word in the original Greek. It means to miss the mark. A man shoots his arrow at a target, and the arrow misses. Sin is the failure to live up to God's standards, to hit the target of life, to be what we ought to be and can be. (2) *Paraptoma,* to trespass. It is taking the wrong road when we could have and should have taken the right one. It is the failure to reach the goal and journey's end we should have reached.

When we take the wrong road or miss the target God has for our lives, our sin impacts us as individuals and trickles down to our families.

10. Rebuilding is about healing relationships with God and with others. Prayerfully look over this family inventory, and put a check mark in front of the characteristics you believe need to be addressed in your family:

____ "perfect family" syndrome
____ denial ("It will go away.")
____ poor communication
____ emotional dependency
____ manipulation and control
____ lack of boundaries

____ lack of same-sex bonding
____ expressing negative opinions about the opposite sex
____ poor marital relationship
____ incest/molestation in the family
____ use of pornography, sexually explicit material
____ uncontrolled anger
____ passivity
____ addictive behaviors, such as alcohol and drug addiction
____ an unattractive image of femininity or masculinity
____ encouraging the child to do nontypical gender activities

11. Which of these characteristics was a surprise to you?

Why?

> "At the very core of our development is the way we learn from infancy to interpret and respond to the significant people in our lives. Since much of our identity is shaped by our attachment pattern and by the reflections we receive from others about who we are, any imperfections that exist in our family members can greatly distort how we interpret our own value and place in the world."
> —David Takle

12. How has generational sin impacted you?

13. What changes in the above areas would most impact your relationship with God?

With your sexually broken loved one?

"Brokenness is the process by which God dislodges our self-life and teaches us to rely upon Him alone in every facet of our lives. . . . The goal, then, of spiritual brokenness is to reduce a Christ-follower's resistance to the flow of God's Spirit through his or her life. . . . God must break us in order to use us."

—Lon Solomon

As you look over this list, you may not fully comprehend how these dynamics have impacted you and your family. Ask God to open your eyes and give you a willing heart to repent of your sins or mistakes and dig deeper in understanding them, especially the ones you checked. Consider making an appointment to speak to a pastor or Christian counselor who can help you with the areas that need healing in your family.

14. Change takes time. Choose one area to work on initially. There is much to learn and develop within us as we seek to find healing and restoration. (For more help, look at "Recommended Reading" on page 119.)

Taking Another Look

Perhaps as you read through the list of family dynamics, you found nothing that applied to your life. You have been a Christian for many years, and God has made many changes in your life already.

Consider this: Maybe God allowed sexual brokenness to enter your home to forever alter your view of yourself, God, others, and life in general. Through the devastating news of homosexuality or transgenderism, God is showing you your heart, putting a mirror, as it were, in front of your life and motivations.

As believers, we speak about how much we love God and desire to serve Him. But what stimulates our service? How many of our good works are driven by human energy, pride, and a desire for recognition? What has been the incentive behind our dreams for our loved ones' success?

The life-crushing reality of family members who struggle with sexual brokenness may rob us of our long-sought-after reputation among our friends and fellow churchgoers. We fear losing their respect. Our pride and religious self-deception make us judge and jury over the sins of our loved ones and other people. We focus on the approval of others, rather than the approval of God.

When God truly breaks us, He brings us to the end of ourselves. He uproots our pride and its deceptive motivation. We no longer live to seek the approval of others but, rather, to glorify God.

15. What is God showing you about yourself in this process of dealing with sexual sin and brokenness?

Surrendering to God

How do we begin to change ourselves and/or our families? *Personal change occurs when we pursue a greater goal than our own selfish desires.* Transformation begins with a total commitment to Jesus Christ and surrender to His will in our lives. It is a death to self.

But what if our loved ones never change? What if we can never help them? What if they die of AIDS? Relinquishing ourselves and our loved ones to God will bring peace and the knowledge that we are safe in His hands. He will guide us on this painful journey, which is full of unanswered questions and unfulfilled dreams. We can believe His Word is true and trust that His intentions for us and our loved ones are good.

However, change in our loved ones will depend on their choices. We can partner with God by praying that they will see the futility of their decisions and be willing to follow His will. But, ultimately, the determination to change is theirs.

Will you pray this prayer of commitment to God?

> *Dear heavenly Father,*
>
> *I confess that I have been full of pride and self-sufficiency. You said that "pride goes before destruction, a haughty spirit before a fall" (Proverbs 16:18). I have wanted to serve You, but I have wanted to do it on my own terms. I have believed that I could handle this trial of sexual sin by myself, by my own knowledge and resources. I confess I have not fully trusted You, causing me to resist turning my loved one over to You. I confess I have sinned by placing my will and my desires above Yours.*
>
> *I ask your forgiveness for my stubbornness and foolish pride. I surrender my life, the life of _____ [name of loved one], and the rest of my family completely to You. I acknowledge You as Lord of my life and ask that You guide me, so I will do nothing out of pride and selfishness. I leave the future in Your hands.*
>
> *In the name of Jesus Christ, my Lord and Savior, amen.*

Going Beyond Your Family

The problem of homosexual and transgender behavior is much greater than what is happening within our own families. The church at large, as well as the culture, is experiencing the impact of declining moral standards. God did not allow us into the world of broken sexuality only for ourselves. Our testimonies and our voices must be heard. God does not want us to remain silent in the prison of guilt and shame. He can give us the grace and courage to impact the church and culture if we are willing.

> "Surely it was for my benefit that I suffered such anguish. In your love you kept me from the pit of destruction; you have put all my sins behind your back."
> —Isaiah 38:17

16. When did you tell your pastor about your gay or transgendered loved one? If you haven't, when will you?

17. How can you assist your church or community in knowing how to respond to homosexuality and transgenderism?

18. How do you see yourself having a role in changing the "kingdom of sexual brokenness"?

If not, why not?

REBUILDING

Choose one of the family dynamics from the list on pages 70–71 that is unfamiliar to you. Do some research online, go to the library, or talk with a counselor about it. From your findings, write below how that particular characteristic might impact a family. Prepare to report your findings to your small group, or discuss them with your spouse.

Memorize Isaiah 38:17.

8

DEALING WITH THE OPPOSITION

The Sunday-school room was filling with families exchanging greetings and chatting with one another as they entered. As the support group was about to begin, Jean and Phil came in and found a place at the far end of the circle.

When it was Jean's turn to speak, she told the group, "My son, Robert, was the music pastor of a large church. He was married and is the father of our precious granddaughter, Evie.

"Robert told me he had been counseling Ryan, a 15-year-old boy in their church. He was just trying to help the young man because he understood his struggle with same-sex attractions.

"'However,' Robert said, 'when Ryan wanted a kiss from me, I complied.' Ryan's family filed charges. As a result, he was fired from his job and brought up in the court as a sex offender.

"We have been so brokenhearted over it and cannot understand why it has happened. He is so talented, so gifted musically. What's even worse, Robert decided he was tired of keeping the secret of his same-sex attractions and separated from our daughter-in-law, leaving Evie without her daddy. It has been so hard on all of us."

Phil picked up the conversation. "But I have to tell you that Robert explained a lot to us this week, and we understand much better where he is coming from. He never wanted to be gay. He even explained to us that the Bible isn't against homosexuality. Jesus never mentioned it, so it must be okay.

"Don't copy the behavior and customs of this world, but let God transform you into a new person by changing the way you think."
—Romans 12:2, NLT

"Victory begins with the name of Jesus on your lips, but it will not be consummated until the nature of Jesus is in your heart."
—Francis Frangipane

"'A servant is not greater than his master. If they persecuted me, they will persecute you also.'"
—John 15:20

"'Blessed are you when people insult you, persecute you and falsely say all kinds of evil against you because of me. Rejoice and be glad, because great is your reward in heaven.'"
—Matthew 5:11-12

"He also said there is no such thing as a 'homosexual agenda.' All they want is equal rights. It has left us pretty confused."

REFLECTING

How would you describe the politically correct view of homosexuality?

"For a son dishonors his father, a daughter rises up against her mother, a daughter-in-law against her mother-in-law—a man's enemies are the members of his own household."
—Micah 7:6

In what way does your desire to defend your loved one impact your opinions?

EXPLORING

Opposition to following God isn't new. Nehemiah dealt with it, too, when he started rebuilding the walls around Jerusalem.

1. Read Nehemiah 4:1-3. What kind of opposition did Nehemiah face?

"Romans 7:23 and 8:5-7 show that the center of all spiritual bondage is the mind. That's where the battle must be fought and won if you are to experience the freedom in Christ which is your inheritance."
—Neil T. Anderson

Why? (See Ezra 4:6-13 for a similar situation when the Jewish people were rebuilding the Temple and walls of Jerusalem.)

2. When have you experienced opposition within your family?

What influenced it?

The taunts that came out of the mouths of Sanballet and Tobiah were painful and discouraging. Their question, "Can they bring stones back to life from those heaps of rubble—burned as they are?" is a physical picture of an emotional condition. It also applies to those of us who have been terribly wounded by the gender confusion of a loved one.

Sanballet and Tobiah used ridicule, insults, mockery, taunting, humiliation, and sarcasm, methods that often are used against believers, especially regarding homosexuality and transgenderism.

3. Give an example of some demoralizing taunts you have heard on television or observed in the newspaper.

4. How have people demoralized or discouraged you on your journey with your loved one?

> "'Do not be afraid or discouraged because of this vast army. For the battle is not yours, but God's. You will not have to fight this battle. Take up your positions; stand firm and see the deliverance the LORD will give you.'"
> —2 Chronicles 20:15, 17

> "Behold, You desire truth in the innermost being, and in the hidden part You will make me know wisdom."
> —Psalm 51:6, NASB

> "The more we see the pervasiveness of deception, the more hope there is that life can be different."
> —David Takle

Challenge to Our Faith

In our desire to remain faithful to God in our journey with homosexuality, we may experience opposition from our loved ones who struggle, as well as from friends and other influential people.

In Nehemiah's situation, the enemy was visible; and the battle for Jerusalem was physical. With homosexuality and transgenderism, the enemy is not our loved ones. It is Satan, and the battle is spiritual. Satan deceives our loved ones and, in our sympathy and love for them, tempts

"We are where we are and what we are because of what has gone into our minds. We change where we are and what we are by changing what goes into our minds."
—Zig Ziglar

"Let us realize, therefore, that the *energies we expend in keeping our sins secret are the actual 'materials' of which a stronghold is made. The demon you are fighting is actually using your thoughts to protect his access to your life.*"
—Francis Frangipane

"Because we are Christians the devil is unusually active with respect to us; and therefore of all people we should be the least surprised when these things happen to us."
—D. Martyn Lloyd-Jones

us to believe those same lies. It is a battle for our minds, rather than our bodies.

Imagine our loved ones being like Trojan horses. On the outside, we know them and believe they are familiar and trustworthy. But if they have given over their minds to the lies about their gender or sexuality, they now bring with them the deceptions of the enemy of our souls. How cunning those falsehoods can be when presented by beloved family members! Our natural response is to defend and protect our loved ones, which has been our action in the past. Particularly, if we have seen the pain our loved ones have experienced, it is easier to want them to be happy, rather than to be holy.

5. What is one thing your loved one has told you that you wish you could believe?

6. What have you learned that is confusing to you?

Preparation for Warfare

When we are dealing with sexual brokenness in the home, it is tempting to argue with our loved ones that homosexual or transgender relationships are not healthy or stable. And, yes, that is true. A careful examination of the research can reveal statistics that are undisputed even in the LGBT community.

Despite all the facts documented through research and experience, people who are same-sex attracted or transgender have difficulty accepting the reality of negative consequences. It also does not prevent them from getting more deeply involved. As Sy Rogers, a recovered homosexual, explained, "Bad love is better than no love at all."

7. What good or bad changes have you seen in your loved one's homosexual or transgender behavior?

8. What influences him or her the most?

Battle for the Mind

At the core of same-sex attraction is a desperate need to be loved and affirmed by someone of the same gender. Many factors impact this phenomenon. Neglect, various abusive or traumatic experiences, lack of bonding with a same-sex parent, and cultural influences together can create a void that longs to be filled. As sexually broken people continue to convince themselves that their feelings are accurate, they act out; and the pleasurable behavior gradually becomes addictive.

9. Read Romans 1:24-28. How did Paul describe this kind of thinking?

"So, if you think you are standing firm, be careful that you don't fall! No temptation has overtaken you except what is common to mankind. And God is faithful; he will not let you be tempted beyond what you can bear. But when you are tempted, he will also provide a way out so that you can endure it."
—1 Corinthians 10:12-13

"If we *tolerate* darkness through tolerance of sin, we leave ourselves vulnerable to satanic assault. For wherever there is willful disobedience to the Word of God, there is spiritual darkness and the potential for demonic activity."
—Francis Frangipane

No one knows the exact causes of homosexuality or transgenderism. We do know we are sinners from the time of our conception (Psalm 51:5). We also know God designed us male or female, and going against God's blueprint for our gender or sexuality is sin. Looking more deeply, we see abuse, betrayal, and rejection giving fertile soil to this rejection of God's plan for our lives.

> "Every battle we face in life is over the Word and whether or not we can build our lives upon the faithfulness and integrity of God."
> —Francis Frangipane

> "Fear God and keep his commandments, for this is the duty of all mankind. For God will bring every deed into judgment, including every hidden thing, whether it is good or evil."
> —Ecclesiastes 12:13-14

> "But now that you have been set free from sin and have become slaves of God, the benefit you reap leads to holiness, and the result is eternal life. For the wages of sin is death, but the gift of God is eternal life in Christ Jesus our Lord."
> —Romans 6:22-23

10. What lies does your loved one believe about him or herself?

11. What lies have you believed in your journey with your loved one?

Deception of the Heart

The "heart" of the homosexual or transgender person houses the mind, will, and emotions and becomes deeply wounded through life experiences. The emotional damage affects the mind (or the heart's belief system) and concludes over time that same-sex behavior or opposite gender change is attractive and tolerable. When combined with one's sinful, rebellious human nature, individuals succumb to deception about their sexual or gender identity.

What influences our minds and hearts regulates our belief systems. These beliefs determine our behavior. In order for us to change our behavior, our minds and thoughts must be conformed to God's truth as found in His Word.

12. Read Romans 12:1-2. How does Scripture say we should we respond to lies about sexual brokenness?

Our minds and hearts, as well as those of our loved ones, can be darkened by deception. We internalize rejection and bitterness; so we must rely on God, the great Surgeon, to operate on our hearts, opening us up to His love and mercy. Our role is to pray for God to bring about a transformation of our minds and hearts, as well as those of our loved ones.

Does that mean our loved ones will become heterosexual? Or our transgender family members will change? The experiences that have so deeply impacted them are not easily forgotten, but God can redeem their wounding. It's important to remember that the opposite of ungodly sexual behaviors is not heterosexuality but the pursuit of holiness. When Jesus is Lord of our lives, sexual brokenness can be overcome.

13. What negative experiences may have played a part in deceiving your heart or the heart of your family member?

Proverbs 4:23 says, "Above all else, guard your heart." Just as our homosexual or transgendered loved ones have been deceived, we, too, can buy into lies. Our hearts are broken by our loved ones' pain and sexual brokenness. We can get discouraged and think God is not working. We fear losing the relationship and begin to compromise our standards. Perhaps we get tired of the nagging guilt that pursues us. We get weary of standing for what is right. Or we may begin to question the authority of Scripture and become persuaded by pro-gay theology.

No matter how these temptations come, Satan will work hard to destroy our faith in God, destroy our families, and destroy our homosexual or transgendered loved ones. His favorite tool is discouragement. And he likes to make us think

"When tempted, no one should say, 'God is tempting me.' For God cannot be tempted by evil, nor does he tempt anyone; but each person is tempted when they are dragged away by their own evil desire and enticed. Then, after desire has conceived, it gives birth to sin; and sin, when it is full-grown, gives birth to death."
—James 1:13-15

"Although we cannot alter the past, we can put our past upon the 'altar' as an act of worship. A worshipping heart truly allows God to restore the soul."
—Francis Frangipane

"The negative results of sinful actions are one of the strongest deterrents to continued sin. So don't pray that God will remove the consequences of your child's sinful behavior— and don't thwart God's purposes by removing them yourself."
—Anita Worthen and Bob Davies

> "'But the things that come out of a person's mouth come from the heart, and these defile them. For out of the heart come evil thoughts—murder, adultery, sexual immorality, theft, false testimony, slander.'"
> —Matthew 15:18-19

> "Temptation comes to me, suggesting a possible shortcut to the realization of my highest goal—it does not direct me toward what I understand to be evil, but toward what I understand to be good. . . . When I yield to it, I have made lust a god."
> —Oswald Chambers

> "See to it, brothers and sisters, that none of you has a sinful, unbelieving heart that turns away from the living God. But encourage one another daily, . . . so that none of you may be hardened by sin's deceitfulness."
> —Hebrews 3:12-13

God has abandoned us or our loved ones. His greatest joy is to slander God's reputation and destroy our relationship with Him.

14. What deception is playing havoc with your heart right now?

No family is without problems. The last perfect parent was God. He placed His children, Adam and Eve, in the Garden of Eden, an unspoiled paradise. He made sure all their needs were met and made it possible for them to have perfect companionship with each other and with Him. Their circumstances could not have been better. Yet, when Satan entered the picture, Adam and Eve yielded to temptation and sinned against God.

Their struggle with sin is the same as ours. Satan appears shrewd in his arguments, making us think our rebellion is nothing more than innocent self-interest. Since that time, he continues to use the same tactics in the way he deceives.

Tactic 1: "Did God really say?" (Genesis 3:1)

Satan wanted Eve to question what God told her. Satan will encourage you to question the Bible and its position on homosexuality and transgenderism. But God's Word has much to say about His divine intent for human sexuality, beginning with Genesis 1 and 2. ("See Sexual Brokenness: A Biblical Perspective" on page 127.) These chapters in Genesis record God creating man in His own image, then creating woman as his helpmate. God created both sexes to be complementary and counterparts of each other. His intent from the beginning was heterosexual, monogamous marriage.

Nothing is vague about God's intent for human sexuality. Both homosexuality and transgender issues go against God's Word and His plan for humanity. While same-sex attractions or gender confusion are not chosen, ungodly behavior is. (See "Sexual Brokenness: A Biblical Perspective" on page 127.)

In the New Testament, Jesus taught only two options for sexual behavior: heterosexual, monogamous marriage or celibacy. Any sexual behavior outside heterosexual marriage is against His will. Jesus also had great compassion for sinners, calling them to repentance and righteousness. Through His death on the cross, He paid the price for sin and gave individuals the power to overcome hard struggles.

Various scholars have explained away many Scripture verses or redefined their meaning. Their conclusion is that the Bible doesn't condemn homosexuality or transgenderism. Their theology is not so much about making homosexuality acceptable as it is about destroying the authority of Scripture. (See *The Gay Gospel?* by Joe Dallas.) If we do not have solid footing in God's Word, any sin can be acceptable in our eyes. We must never surrender our faith in the authority of God's Word.

15. Which arguments that defend homosexual or transgender behavior have you heard from your loved one?

> "Because he himself suffered when he was tempted, he is able to help those who are being tempted."
> —Hebrews 2:18

> "For though we live in the world, we do not wage war as the world does. The weapons we fight with are not the weapons of the world. On the contrary, they have divine power to demolish strongholds. We demolish arguments and every pretension that sets itself up against the knowledge of God, and *we take captive every thought to make it obedient to Christ.*"
> —2 Corinthians 10:3-5, emphasis added

Draw an arrow in front of the one you are most tempted to believe.

Tactic 2: *"You will not certainly die" (Genesis 3:4)*

Satan denied God's specific command: "You must not eat from the tree of the knowledge of good and evil, for when you eat from it you will certainly die" (Genesis 2:17). God's intent and will for Adam and Eve was life. Eve's action indicated she trusted Satan's lie, rather than God's truth.

As Scripture progresses, it becomes clear that death did enter their lives—death of innocence; death of their unbroken fellowship with God; death of the harmony in their relationship with each other; and, eventually, physical death. Real consequences come with wrong choices.

"So then, just as you received Christ Jesus as Lord, continue to live your lives in him, rooted and built up in him, strengthened in the faith as you were taught, and overflowing with thankfulness. See to it that no one takes you captive through hollow and deceptive philosophy, which depends on human tradition and the elemental spiritual forces of this world rather than on Christ."
—Colossians 2:6-8

Homosexuality and transgenderism are among many sins addressed in Scripture. They fall under the classification of immoral sexual behavior. But because the Bible addresses numerous sins, it is easy to believe one is no worse than another or "We all sin, so it shouldn't matter." The question is not the nature of our sin but what we are going to do with the sin when God makes it clear He does not want us to disobey Him.

16. The good news is that God can and does redeem homosexual—and transgender—people. Read 1 Corinthians 6:9-11. What is your initial reaction to these verses?

What do these verses do for your hope in your situation?

17. What kind of temptations are most troubling in your life or in the life of your sexually broken loved one?

18. What works to help you overcome temptation?

Tactic 3: "You will be like God" (Genesis 3:5)

Satan suggested to Eve that God was withholding a good thing from her out of selfish motives. Satan implied she could eat from the tree of the knowledge of good and evil and also have the same wisdom God had.

By defying God's commandment, Adam and Eve sought to be morally independent from God. In other words, they could make their own decisions about what was right and wrong and live life without obeying God or His commands.

For us or for our homosexual or transgendered loved ones, God can seem unfair. We do not choose our feelings or attractions. Why would God require that we live within His monogamous, heterosexual boundaries for humanity?

The longing to be loved and accepted is universal. Practicing homosexuality or giving in to gender dysphoria temporarily fulfills broken dreams. As a result, human idols are created that reject God the Creator and worship and serve created beings (Romans 1:25). By twisting Scripture and reinterpreting various passages that have stood for thousands of years, proponents of these behaviors, in essence, set themselves up as gods and worship idols of their own making.

Eve yielded to temptation in order to satisfy a perceived human need (hunger), then she encouraged Adam to do the same. Her disobedience came out of her desire to do her own thing and make her own decision, even when God told her and Adam not to eat the fruit of that tree. Adam and Eve disobeyed God and took a bite of the fruit because it was (1) "good for food," (2) "pleasing to the eye," and (3) "desirable for gaining wisdom" (Genesis 3:6), three ways Satan entices the human heart. In reality, they were rebelling against God's command.

Every sin, whether it is yours or your family member's, starts with temptation and ends in rebellion against God. Eventually, people become slaves to their sin and cannot easily escape. Only God's power can make the difference.

> "Why are our wounds most vulnerable to sin? Because when we hurt, we try to assuage our pain, and almost every method that we use *by ourselves* conforms to what the Bible calls sin. For example, when struck by others, literally or symbolically, we either strike back—using revenge as a substitute for healing; or we strike back at our own hurting selves, soothing the pain with sex, drugs, or any heightened stimulation—substituting pleasure for genuine peace."
> —Dr. Jeffrey Satinover

19. Which one of the above three temptations is the easiest for you to succumb to?

20. Which of the above temptations might your loved one be dealing with?

How does the knowledge of this temptation help you understand him or her better?

REBUILDING

Our thought lives comprise who we are, so we must first be honest about our own unbelief, temptations, pride, unforgiveness, etc. Just because we are Christians does not mean we are perfect. It is important to humble ourselves and admit we need help.

Next, we must look objectively at our thought lives. Are my thoughts and attitudes conformed to Jesus' teachings? Am I entertaining thoughts that are not pleasing to God?

What we do with our thoughts determines our ability to grow and mature in Christ. If thoughts come that are not from God, we must put them under Christ's authority and expel them from our minds, so Satan will not get a foothold in our lives.

The following questions will help you know whether or not your thoughts are coming from God or Satan:

- Is this thought consistent with who God is and what He says in His Word?
- Does this thought protect and nurture my life?
- Will this thought keep me out of sinful behavior?
- Does this thought help me meet my goal of becoming more like Christ?

What can you do to remember to ask yourself these questions when you are tempted? To whom can you be accountable to do so? Write your action plan below.

Memorize Colossians 2:6-8.

9

FIGHTING FOR OUR LOVED ONES

Robert was in trouble. Busted. His magazine stash had been discovered. His mother had been cleaning his room and found it hidden under his dirty clothes in the closet. Now he had to tell his parents the truth.

He sat down at the desk in his room, briefly looking up at the moonlight streaming through the window. He opened his laptop and started writing a letter.

Dear Mom and Dad,

Yes, I know what this is all about. You found the gay magazines and videos in my closet. No, I don't have anything to say for myself. Even if I did, I wouldn't know where to begin. Yes, I know they are full of trash. And no, you didn't raise me this way.

Why haven't you asked me your real concern yet? I can see you're burning to. I've always kept Playboys *and* Hustlers *mixed in with my stash so, in the event you stumbled on to it, you wouldn't think I'm gay. But yes, Mom and Dad, I am gay. At least I think I am. I've been attracted to men ever since I can recall.*

Please believe me, I'm not some pervert. I'm not promiscuous. In fact, I would have chosen any number of problems before choosing to be gay. I just like men. I have always liked men and cannot remember ever not liking men. The truth is I just grew up gay. I felt attracted to men way before I even knew what sex was.

Mom, Dad, I know how difficult this may be for you. I've always feared my little secret being revealed more than I fear death itself. But, you know something? Now that you both know,

"Be alert and of sober mind. Your enemy the devil prowls around like a roaring lion looking for someone to devour. Resist him, standing firm in the faith, because you know that the family of believers throughout the world is undergoing the same kind of sufferings."
—1 Peter 5:8-9

"He is no fool who gives what he cannot keep to gain that which he cannot lose."
—Jim Elliott

"If you do not stand firm in your faith, you will not stand at all."
—Isaiah 7:9

"Do not be afraid of them; the LORD your God himself will fight for you."
—Deuteronomy 3:22

I don't want to run and hide. I want to tell you more. I want you to understand the isolation, the anxiety and the depression that has kept me behind closed doors and antisocial all these years. It was never because I didn't love you. Many times I would just close my bedroom door, turn up the volume on my radio, and cry. Sometimes for hours.

I know I haven't been the best son in the world. It's not easy to love others when you hate yourself. But after telling you the truth, I feel, for the first time, a sense of relief. Desperately. You see, Mom and Dad, I hate being gay. If there were a way out, I'd grab it in a heartbeat.

"Blessed are you when people insult you, persecute you and falsely say all kinds of evil against you because of me. Rejoice and be glad, because great is your reward in heaven."
—Matthew 5:11-12

Maybe, just maybe, God led you to find my stash. Every night for the past ten years, I've been praying for help. I hate my life the way it is and will cooperate 100% if you'll help me out of this hell. ***Please don't be politically correct and tell me that you accept my sexual orientation and will always love me. Even if you loved me gay, I would not.***

No. I'm tired of the lusting, the secrecy, and the anxiety. Please help me to find a way out. I love you, Mom and Dad. I'll be in my room.

Love, Your Son

REFLECTING

"Pray for a good harvest, but keep on hoeing."
—Slovenian Proverb

What kind of opposition is Roger experiencing in his journey with sexual brokenness in the family?

"No one is hopeless who hopes in God."
—David C. McCasland

Has your loved one asked you for help in his or her struggle?

If so, how have you handled this request?

EXPLORING

Whenever we attempt to follow God's will, we will encounter opposition. Satan does not want healing and transformation to happen. Nehemiah, too, faced conflict and discouragement. When he first informed the exiles of his plan to rebuild Jerusalem, they appeared to be enthusiastic. He had a plan, the needed materials, and the support of the King. So "the people worked with all their heart" (Nehemiah 4:6). However, when they faced the enemy forces, who were out to stir up trouble, their courage and determination was challenged.

1. Read Nehemiah 4:7-17. How did Sanballat, Tobiah, and others react to the building project?

2. What was Nehemiah's response to their reaction?

3. How did the Jewish people respond?

4. Why wasn't Nehemiah discouraged with the opposition?

Our Discouragement

When we are dealing with a sexually broken person in the family, the initial enthusiasm we may have for change, including the family being rebuilt, can cool quickly. Whatever the damage that came to our loved one is complex and difficult to

"We do not want you to be uninformed, brothers and sisters, about the troubles we experienced in the province of Asia. We were under great pressure, far beyond our ability to endure, so that we despaired of life itself. Indeed, we felt we had received the sentence of death. But this happened that we might not rely on ourselves but on God, who raises the dead. He has delivered us from such a deadly peril, and he will deliver us again. On him we have set our hope that he will continue to deliver us."
—2 Corinthians 1:8-10

"Prayer is an act of partnership with God. . . . Prayer is primarily an act of spiritual warfare, an enormous threat to Satan's plans. For when we take the authority God has given us to exercise the privileges of our relationship with Him by calling on Him in prayer, the enemy is in trouble."
—Charles Kraft

91

"Unless the Lord builds the house, the builders labor in vain. Unless the Lord watches over the city, the guards stand watch in vain."
—Psalm 127:1

"Whenever we pray with hope, we put our lives in the hands of God. Fear and anxiety fade away, and everything we are given and everything we are deprived of is nothing but a finger pointing out the direction of God's hidden promise that one day we shall taste in full."
—Henri J. M. Nouwen

"Relinquishment is giving someone up; abandonment is giving up on someone. There is a big difference. When we let go of our loved ones, we stop taking responsibility *for* them. But we don't stop fulfilling our responsibilities *to* them."
—Anita Worthen and Bob Davies

understand. We may still be angry over the abuse or trauma that was outside our control. We have made mistakes we deeply regret. Other family members may accept or condone the sexual preferences of this family member and strongly oppose our beliefs. The ever-present, pro-LGBT media, which presents homosexuality and transgenderism as normal, seduces the hearts and minds of our loved ones.

Like Nehemiah, it takes effort on our part to rebuild our family—and not everyone will agree that the walls need to be rebuilt. As we stand for moral values and attempt to rebuild the family, it can feel like we are pushing water uphill—a process that is overwhelming and discouraging!

5. What have you experienced lately that has been particularly discouraging to you?

6. How often have you entertained what it would mean to give up on your family member?

If you did, what would the spiritual impact be on you and the rest of your family?

Nehemiah's Challenge

Nehemiah was only one man. He was facing tremendous odds. Not only did he have to fight real enemies, he had to encourage his own troops and prevent them from quitting. If we take a look at what kept Nehemiah going, we can understand what might help us.

7. What kept Nehemiah moving forward?

Prayer

Prayer was the guiding light of Nehemiah's life. Throughout the entire story, we see him turning to God to pray. He prayed when he heard the bad news. He prayed and fasted to find out what God wanted him to do. He prayed before he informed the king of his needs and desires. And he prayed in the face of the battle.

He did not make decisions or move into action until he first prayed. Nehemiah knew he had to rely on God if he and his people were going to finish rebuilding the walls. He knew prayer took humility and dependence on God. He was willing to acknowledge that God could do what he could not.

Prayer is letting go of control, letting go of our sense of security in what we know, what is familiar, and believing that the God of the universe will do what He deems best. It is trusting God even when the circumstances appear to be against us. When nothing seems to be happening, God is happening.

Prayer is the only way the minds of our loved ones can be reached. Sexual brokenness is not about sex. It is about a need to be loved, and Satan has taken this legitimate need and twisted it into a perversion of God's desires for humanity.

8. What makes it difficult for you to pray about your situation? (See "Prayers for Prodigals" on page 125.)

"Though he brings grief, he will show compassion, so great is his unfailing love. For he does not willingly bring affliction or grief to anyone."
—Lamentations 3:32-33

"'I have loved you with an everlasting love; I have drawn you with unfailing kindness. I will build you up again.'"
—Jeremiah 31:3-4

"'Come, all you who are thirsty, come to the waters; and you who have no money, come buy and eat! Give ear and come to me; listen that you may live.'"
—Isaiah 55:1, 3

Persuasion

Nehemiah knew he was doing God's will. Having come from Jewish roots, he knew God had given his people the land through His promise to Abraham. The land belonged to his ancestors, the twelve tribes of Israel. And it was up to him and others to reclaim it, rebuild it, and protect it from further deterioration.

"If either of them falls down, one can help the other up. But pity anyone who falls and has no one to help them up. Also, if two lie down together, they will keep warm. But how can one keep warm alone? Though one may be overpowered, two can defend themselves. A cord of three strands is not quickly broken."
—Ecclesiastes 4:10-12

"Have the same mindset as Christ Jesus: Who, being in very nature God, did not consider equality with God something to be used to his own advantage; rather, he made himself nothing by taking the very nature of a servant, being made in human likeness. And being found in appearance as a man, he humbled himself by becoming obedient to death—even death on a cross!"
—Philippians 2:5-8

Nehemiah was persuaded he was not fighting this battle alone. In Jewish history, when God fought to reclaim a portion of the earth that the powers of this world had claimed for themselves, it was referred to as "holy war." Rebuilding the walls of Jerusalem was a holy war, meaning God was the one fighting for the land. All Nehemiah had to do was listen and obey.

Nehemiah believed God was the one who would fight on their behalf, so he addressed his prayer that way: "Turn their insults back on their own heads. Give them over as plunder in the land of captivity" (4:4). This is not the normal way we pray, but it makes sense if we believe God is fighting for us.

Note that Nehemiah did not react directly to Sanballet and Tobiah with ugly remarks or verbal taunting. He channeled his anger to and through God, the Source who could truly do something about the situation.

9. How might dealing with sexual brokenness be like a holy war?

10. How have you handled your anger when someone expresses ugly remarks about your loved one?

What might you do next time?

If we look in Nehemiah 5, we see the secret to Nehemiah's model behavior in verse 15: "But out of reverence for God, I did not act like that." Prayer and reverential fear of God will protect us and prevent us from responding in an ungodly way.

God has given us our families with all their warts and problems. When we go through the stress and strain of having a loved one who struggles with same-sex attractions or gender identity, it is easy to give in and give up. Satan continues to badger and discourage us. We want to take out our anger on someone—anyone—for relief.

We are in a spiritual battle, a holy war; and God is fighting for us. No family is perfect. The Old Testament, in particular, abounds with stories of dysfunctional families. If our family is to survive, we must seek God with all our hearts and follow His will. God has promised to fight for us if we will follow Him in humility and obedience.

> "Delight yourself in the LORD; and He will give you the desires of your heart. Commit your way to the LORD, trust also in Him, and He will do it."
> —Psalm 37:4-5, NASB

> "Ultimately, a person's freedom or deliverance from homosexuality comes from a Person, rather than a method."
> —Pastor Phillip Lee

11. Sometimes the "rubble" in our family seems so great we are not even sure we want to rebuild. How does your weariness manifest itself?

12. Look for a Scripture verse that will remind you of God's will for your family and the fact that He is fighting for you. Write it here, then memorize it.

Passion

Nehemiah was passionate about rebuilding the walls because he loved Jerusalem. But He loved God more and knew he was fighting on behalf of God's interests. God called *him* to do the work, so he must remain strong in fulfilling God's will. He invested a great deal in the rebuilding. He had the support and confidence of the King (both King Artaxerxes and his Savior King), the materials to rebuild, and God's blessing on his efforts.

> "Whenever we find ourselves tending to be discouraged, and to feel that we have a sense of complaint and of grudge that the Lord does not seem to be fulfilling His promises to us, that very moment we must heed this exhortation to 'Stand!' 'Pull yourself together,' 'brace yourself up.' We must not give way to the self-pitying thoughts that come crowding into our mind and heart. As Christians we should never feel sorry for ourselves. . . . The moment we do so, we lose our energy, we lose the will to fight, and the will to live, and are paralysed."
> —D. Martyn Lloyd-Jones

Nehemiah could have given in to his emotions. He could have been bitter at his own people who were losing strength and wanting to walk away. He could have quit. But his love for God and his call to do the work kept him moving forward. His reverent fear of God kept him from retreating or turning back.

Sometimes our families are so broken we want to disown them. Our passion to see change results in weariness and discouragement when it doesn't happen quickly enough. In our moments of fantasy, we wish we could walk away and belong to another gene pool. The rubble of life has made our families so conflicted we want to quit trying to build relationships.

Isn't it good that God doesn't respond to us that way? "Do you not know? Have you not heard? The LORD is the everlasting God, the Creator of the ends of the earth. He will not grow tired or weary, and his understanding no one can fathom" (Isaiah 40:28). His amazing love continues to probe deeply into our hearts and invites us to come enjoy His presence and rest in Him.

13. How can you rekindle your passion for rebuilding the relationship with your loved one?

With your family?

Sometimes our passion for a loved one becomes more important than our relationship with God. We fear losing him or her totally, so we forsake the authority of God and Scripture in order to approve what our loved one is doing. Instead of standing for God and His truth, we get to the place where we give in, roll over, and approve of sexually broken behavior. We are tempted to elevate the relationship with our loved one above the holy life God has called us to.

14. What are some of the temptations that have come to your mind about accepting and approving of your loved one's sexual or gender-conflicted behavior?

> "If you seek a heart that does not condemn, if you crucify your instinct to judge, you will have laid a true foundation for the gift of discernment, for you will have prepared your heart to receive the dreams, visions and insights from God. You will be unstained by human bias and corruption."
> —Francis Frangipane

15. When do you find yourself most tempted to "throw in the towel"?

> "The word of God is alive and active. Sharper than any double-edged sword, it penetrates even to dividing soul and spirit, joints and marrow; it judges the thoughts and attitudes of the heart."
> —Hebrews 4:12

Plan

Nehemiah was unwilling to give in and let his enemies fulfill their evil intent. He realized he was not in a personal war; he was in a holy war. He was engaged in the battle with God against Satan, who wished to destroy the Jewish people. He went to God for His orders and took specific measures to protect his people and the progress they were making on the walls.

Nehemiah made a plan to defend the work. He first posted a guard who was assigned to serve a twenty-four-hour shift. Then he assigned people behind the lowest points of the wall, their most vulnerable positions. Entire families served together with the appropriate weapons—swords, spears, and bows. He encouraged the people by reminding them to remember that God was fighting for them.

He divided the men between the doers and the defenders. Even for those who did the work, a sword was always at their side. Lastly, he assigned a man who would blow the trumpet. The trumpet call was a signal to gather together at the specific location along the wall. "Join us there," Nehemiah said. "Our God will fight for us!"

It is the nature of spiritual warfare that we cannot rest while we are in the battle. We must not fight alone. Satan will attack us when and where we are most vulnerable.

> "Therefore, prepare your minds for action; be self-controlled; set your hope fully on the grace to be given you when Jesus Christ is revealed."
> —1 Peter 1:13

16. Have you found other families who are fighting the same battle? If so, how are you supporting one another?

If not, when and where will you begin to look for other people to support you?

REBUILDING

Neil T. Anderson and Rich Miller, in their book *Walking in Freedom: 21 Days to Securing Your Identity in Christ*, describe when we are most susceptible to temptation. They use the acrostic BLASTED—bored, lonely, angry, self-pitying, tired, extra-stressed, or depressed. During these emotional times, we will be the most tempted to give in to our flesh and quit standing for God.

We, too, are in a holy war. Satan has taken ground in the lives of our loved ones, and God wants us to remain in the battle with Him.

Satan's tactic is to keep us hopeless and overwhelmed, fighting single-handedly. God made us to be in relationship, to carry one another's burdens. Posting watchmen on the wall is the same as asking people to pray with us, to see the enemy we cannot see, to warn us of the coming storm.

Asking friends and family members to join us in this battle is God's intent. He knows we cannot carry this burden alone. We need to surround ourselves with other individuals and families who are dealing with this issue and can bring us comfort and mutual prayer support.

The trumpet was a symbol of the Lord's presence. It was a rallying cry for the people, an indication that God was present and fighting for them. When we have new challenges with our sexually broken loved ones, new situations that are out of our control, we can sound the "trumpet," asking our prayer warriors to pray with us.

What prayer partners do you have supporting you in this battle? Make a list, and ask permission to call them when you need prayer.

What did you learn from Nehemiah's plan that can help you?

Memorize 1 Peter 5:8-9.

10

PUTTING ON GOD'S ARMOR

Jim opened his eyes. For a moment, he couldn't remember why he spent the night on the sofa. Rubbing the back of his neck, he stood and stretched. "Ouch!" he said. "That arm didn't make much of a pillow."

He pushed on the bedroom door. Crumpled tissues dotted the floor. Patti was still asleep, so Jim headed for the kitchen to make coffee. "I'll shower, then take her a cup," he said to himself as he glanced at his watch. "Thank God, Andy will be here in less than an hour." A pastor and good friend from college days, Andy was their go-to person anytime they were having problems.

> "But since we belong to the day, let us be sober, putting on faith and love as a breastplate, and the hope of salvation as a helmet."
> —1 Thessalonians 5:8

Hot water drizzled down Jim's face. Patti wandered into the bathroom in her sweats. "Why didn't you wake me up?" she asked. After splashing her face with cold water, she pulled her normally flawless hairdo into an unkempt ponytail. "I'm making coffee," she said.

"Coffee's already on," Jim yelled. "Andy should be here around 10:00. Maybe you could fix him some of your cinnamon toast."

Patti strolled to the kitchen and looked at the mess. "Thanksgiving must have been a culinary masterpiece," she said to herself as she dropped the cinnamon bread in the toaster. Hurriedly, she packed the dishwasher, hiding the remaining dirty dishes in the oven. Then she returned to the bedroom.

The doorbell rang. "Would you get the door, Jim? I'm putting on some lipstick."

Jim greeted Andy warmly. "Hey, bro. How's it going?" As they settled in the family room, Jim continued. "Thanks for coming by, Andy. You will never know what a godsend you have been to us."

Patti joined them, offering coffee and cinnamon toast. "Hey, Andy," she said, giving him a hug. "It's so good to see you! Did you have a good Thanksgiving?"

"Sure did. How about you?"

"Evil is a personal being. There would be no evil in this world if there were no evil persons; there would be no evil human beings unless there were evil spiritual beings who entered into God's creation and tempted man and seduced him in the calamity of the Fall. The evil state of the world today stems from that calamity."

—D. Martyn Lloyd-Jones

"I'm having a hard time," she said, settling into the recliner. "Jim and I were so excited when Brad asked if he could bring his friend, Trey, home for Thanksgiving. You know Brad hasn't had a lot of boys his age as friends. We thought he had found a good college friend he could really enjoy—only to discover Trey is his gay partner."

"Dinner was awful!" Jim said. "Brad and Trey talked about homosexuality in front of all the family. Everyone became quiet. I think we were all in shock! Brad and Trey excused themselves and left after Patti left the table in tears. What a horrible way to end Thanksgiving dinner. The holiday will never be the same for us."

Andy's words flowed with gentleness. "I'm so sorry you are hurting. It had to be a tough day for you. You know God loves you very much and would not wish for this to happen. I suspect this trial may be one of the hardest you'll ever go through."

Patti, in tears, nodded her head.

Andy continued. "I love you two very much. My love for you and Brad will never change. Brad is a like a son to me. He's a fine young man. You have done your best to be good parents and raise him in the faith and knowledge of Jesus Christ. I have watched him grow up in the church, and I know God's hand is on his life. Your hopes and dreams for Brad seem dashed, I'm sure, but today is not the end of the story. May I share some thoughts with you?"

"Please do," Jim said.

"I don't know how much the two of you know about homosexuality, but I'd like to talk about it from a spiritual perspective. You are in shock, feeling sorrow and anger with Brad at the moment. Your emotions are normal. You wanted and planned so much for his life. Grieving over the death of your dreams takes time. How can you respond to him in love? It may seem impossible at the moment, but it will come.

"In the meantime, you are walking into the arena of a spiritual battle, probably one of the most difficult you will encounter in your lifetime. Your son is not the enemy; Satan is. He would like nothing better than to destroy the life of your son, his siblings, and you. Like a lion on the prowl, he finds endless ways to make you miserable. He will badger you with guilt and shame, whispering what horrible parents you are. In an attempt to turn you against God, he will do anything he can to separate you from Christ and the church. Don't let him.

"You will be tempted to blame one another, Brad's friends, the church, the culture, and a myriad of other things. You will see your son hurting and want to compromise your faith in

God's Word. Friends will accuse you of not loving your son, saying things like, 'Don't you know your son can't help the fact that he was born gay? Why are you giving him a hard time?' Experts will try to convince you homosexuality is inborn and cannot be helped. But don't give up.

"God is willing and faithful to fight for you. He is the King of kings and Lord of lords, and nothing is too hard for Him. Be encouraged by the hope for change as expressed in 1 Corinthians 6:9-11. Remind yourself of the faithfulness and grace of God for Brad. Sin can be forgiven and redeemed. You are not alone. Each day, put on Christ, the armor of God. God is with you, and the battle is His. I pledge to pray for you daily."

REFLECTING

What is your first reaction to Andy's words?

> "Jehoshaphat stood and said, 'Listen to me.... Have faith in the Lord, your God and you will be upheld; have faith in his prophets and you will be successful.... Jehoshaphat appointed men to sing to the LORD and to praise him.... As they began to sing and praise, the LORD set ambushes against the men of Ammon and Moab . . . and they were defeated."
> —2 Chronicles 20:20-22

Describe the reasons you feel the way you do about his words.

EXPLORING

As long as we are Christ-followers and love God, we are in a battle with the forces of evil. Sometimes we are aware of an evil presence or influence in such encounters, and other times we are not. God knew how difficult the sexual identity struggle would be with our loved ones. He spoke through the apostle Paul to teach us how to navigate successfully in the middle of the conflict.

Nehemiah, too, experienced spiritual warfare. Leading the people to rebuild the city walls was met with ridicule, threats, and intimidations. Nehemiah outfitted his people with swords, shields, bows, and armor, making it possible for them to fight at the same time they were rebuilding.

Nehemiah inspired them with these words: "'Don't be afraid of them. Remember the Lord, who is great and awesome, and fight for your families, your sons and your daughters, your wives and your homes'" (Nehemiah 4:14). Note that Nehemiah says we are to fight *for* our family members, not against them.

> "Life isn't about waiting for the storm to pass. It's about learning how to dance in the rain."
> —Vivian Greene

1. What fears or intimidations have you dealt with on your journey with sexual brokenness?

2. Who or what has been an inspiration to keep you going?

Understanding the Armor of God

Nehemiah and his people used physical weapons and armor to fight against their enemies. As Christians, we have the armor of God.

No soldier goes into battle unarmed. Armor protects the fighter from injury and also provides tools for combat. Both are necessary. In Ephesians 6:10-18, the apostle Paul suggests the only way to fight spiritual battles is with God's armor. When he wrote about it, he was in prison and chained to a Roman soldier. His observation of this soldier's uniform may have inspired him to describe the parallel between physical and spiritual combat.

Paul began this passage with "Be strong in the Lord and in his mighty power" (v. 10). Note that Paul did not instruct us to be strong in ourselves or in the church or in our spiritual leaders. To "be strong in the Lord" is to be empowered through our union with God, drawing our strength from Him. We cannot fight in our own strength. We cannot make a difference in our families or in our world without relying on His power. God's power is like "the mighty strength he exerted when he raised Christ from the dead" (Ephesians 1:19). The armor of God is "putting on" Christ Himself: "But put on the Lord Jesus Christ, and make no provision for the flesh in regard to its lusts" (Romans 13:14 NASB).

The phrase *in Christ* and similar terminology occurs at least one hundred sixty-four times in the New Testament (Richard S. Taylor, ed., *Beacon Dictionary of Theology,* Kansas City, MO: Beacon Hill Press of Kansas City, 1983, p. 278). Note that in the first chapter of Ephesians, "in him" and "in Christ" appear repeatedly. (You may want to look at this chapter and count the number of times these phrases are used.) Being in Christ speaks to our union with Him and His involvement in every aspect of our lives. Through the indwelling presence of Christ, the divine permeates our human personality and gives us the needed power to conform our lives to His teachings.

Following Christ is primarily a heart matter. To succeed, our hearts must be set on God alone, desiring knowledge of God's truth and continually seeking to know more, resolving to repent of those sins nearest and dearest to our hearts, and having the courage and determination to persevere to the end. For example, Moses was tested when God called on him to sacrifice his son, Isaac, "your only son whom you love" (Genesis 22:2). Are *you* ready to choose what God says over your precious loved one?

> "'I tell you, my friends, do not be afraid of those who kill the body and after that can do no more. But I will show you whom you should fear: Fear Him who, after the killing of the body, has authority to throw you in hell.'"
> —Luke 12:4-5

To do so, you need to "put on the full armor of God, so that you can take your stand against the devil's schemes. For our struggle is not against flesh and blood, but against the rulers, against the authorities, against the powers of this dark world and against the spiritual forces of evil in the heavenly realms" (Ephesians 6:11-12).

The apostle Paul brought another dimension of influence to our attention: the unseen spiritual world. The devil or Satan (who also goes by other names) and his forces of evil are mentioned more than fifty times in the Bible (*Beacon Dictionary of Theology*, p. 471). Jesus referred to him as "the prince of this world" (John 12:31; 14:30; 16:11). In doing so, He provided insight into Satan's purposes: to compete with God and be above Him (Isaiah 14:12-14), to lie and deceive (John 8:44), to stimulate disobedience against God (Ephesians 2:2), and to destroy God's Kingdom and His people (Ephesians 6:10-18).

Satan's domain is the realm of darkness. In contrast, "God is light; in him there is no darkness at all" (1 John 1:5). Wherever there is deliberate disobedience to God's Word, spiritual darkness sets in and leaves us vulnerable for demonic activity. When sins are exposed and confessed, darkness is turned into light: "But if we walk in the light, as he is in the light, we have fellowship with one another and the blood of Jesus, his son, purifies us from all sin" (1 John 1:7).

We often are blind to the darkness within. Our greatest defense against this blindness is an open and honest heart before God. Pride is the armor of darkness, and God can never fully trust anyone until he or she has been broken of pride: "God opposes the proud, but shows favor to the humble" (James 4: 6).

Sanballet and Tobiah became tools of Satan, mocking and ridiculing Nehemiah (Nehemiah 2:19). But Nehemiah stood strong in the Lord and personally attested that God was alive and active on his behalf: "The God of heaven will give us success" (v. 20). His confident response gave his people the courage to follow his instructions.

Daniel 11:32 (AMP) promises, "the people who [are spiritually mature and] know their God will display strength and take action [to resist]." To do so, we need to put on the armor of God, which consists of several pieces.

"Consider it pure joy, my brothers and sisters, whenever you face trials of many kinds, because you know that the testing of your faith produces perseverance. Let perseverance finish its work so that you may be mature and complete, not lacking anything."
—James 1:2-4

Belt of Truth

The first piece is the belt of truth. In Paul's day, garments hung loosely from the shoulders. When a soldier was preparing for vigorous action, he tied up his loose clothing with a belt, so it would not get in his way. His sword also hung from the belt, making it easily accessible.

The belt of truth represents the key to a successful defense against the enemy. When we rely on God and His Word, we don't have to be afraid, nor do we need to rely on our own wisdom. The Greek word for truth, *aletheia*, means openness, "what is not concealed . . . what is real . . . what can be depended upon. It doesn't fail or disappoint" (*Beacon Dictionary of Theology*, p. 531).

In Exodus 3:14, God told Moses His name: "I AM WHO I AM." His name means utter genuineness and integrity. Jesus is God's truth revealed. "I am the way, the truth and the life. No one comes to the Father except through me" (John 14:6). The Holy Spirit is "the Spirit of truth" (John 15:26). God's Word is truth. John 1:1 says, "In the beginning was the Word, and the Word was with God, and the Word was God." The teachings of God found in Scripture are truth. God's plan for man's salvation is truth. God is the essence of truth. His incorruptibility refers to His perfect and undeviating truthfulness in all His communications to mankind, especially His promises; it is a guarantee of their fulfillment.

True belief in God and His Word are essential for fighting spiritual battles. Knowing God's truth undergirds us; permeates our hearts and minds; and protects us from false authorities, deceptions, and human philosophies. Scripture is foundational to what is true. Jesus said, "'If you hold to my teaching, you are really my disciples. Then you will know the truth, and the truth will set you free" (John 8:31-32).

3. What can you honestly say about your beliefs? Write out a personal faith statement.

"Be all and only for Jesus. Let Him use you without consulting you first."
—Mother Teresa

As we grow in our faith in God, we learn better how to live in truth, integrity, honesty, and purity. God helps us face the truth, speak the truth in love, and live in the truth—His truth. Our belt of truth reminds us that our ability to protect ourselves when under attack starts with God's truth.

Breastplate of Righteousness

The Roman soldier also wore a breastplate that generally extended from the base of his neck to the upper part of his thighs. As part of God's armor, it protected the heart and major organs vital to his life.

To be righteous is to be right, "fair, just, straight, or equal" (*Beacon Dictionary of Theology*, p. 460). Because God is righteous, he conforms to the moral and spiritual laws He has revealed to us. When we receive Jesus Christ as Lord of our lives, God's righteousness becomes ours; and He conforms our lives to Himself through grace.

Because we are not righteous in and of ourselves, we cannot rely on our own righteousness. Our feelings and emotions fluctuate and influence our faith, our judgment, and our handling of relationships. Satan knows how vulnerable we are to our feelings; and he uses them to deceive, discourage, and defeat us. Our attempts at godliness are not sufficient. Confessing our inability to be totally righteous and asking Jesus to protect our hearts, we rest in the breastplate of His righteousness and our faith in Him. "Therefore, there is now no condemnation to those who are in Christ Jesus" (Romans 8:1).

4. When have you attempted to live a righteous life without God's help?

> "Therefore, since we have been justified through faith, we have peace with God through our Lord Jesus Christ, through whom we have gained access by faith into this grace in which we now stand. And we boast in the hope of the glory of God. Not only so, but we also glory in our sufferings, because we know that suffering produces perseverance; perseverance, character; and character, hope. And hope does not put us to shame, because God's love has poured out into our hearts through the Holy Spirit, who has been given to us."
> —Romans 5:1-5

What was the result?

Shoes of Peace

Roman soldiers wore thick leather sandals with straps. The soles had hobnails and studs underneath to protect against traps or spikes planted in the ground by the enemy. Consequently, the soldier's foot held firmly, so he would not slide, slip, or fall.

Shoes of peace symbolize the assurance of our salvation through our commitment to Jesus Christ. Knowing our sins are forgiven brings wonderful peace and stability into our lives. When God instructs us to stand, our promptness and readiness come from having authentic peace with Him. He gives us confidence and assurance to face the enemy. No longer are we filled with guilt, anxiety, or hostility. "How beautiful on the mountains are the feet of those who bring good news, who proclaim peace, who bring good tidings, who proclaim salvation" (Isaiah 52:7).

5. Read 1 Corinthians 15:1-4. Which phrase from these verses stands out to you?

Why?

> "Those who live according to the flesh have their minds set on what the flesh desires; but those who live in accordance with the Spirit have their minds set on what the Spirit desires."
> —Romans 8:5

Shield of Faith

The soldier's shield hid most of the body. Constructed from two pieces of board glued together and covered with a fireproof metal lining, it was made specifically to quench fiery darts.

Jesus, our Shield of faith, protects us from Satan's barrage of "fiery darts." Fiery darts start in the realm of our thoughts. Satan's strategy prevents us from understanding that he is the cause of these thoughts. Temptations, blasphemous thoughts about God, words, phrases, oaths, and horrible language come into our minds and hearts and fool us into believing these thoughts are our own. We question whether we are truly Christians. Fear and condemnation fill our minds and hearts.

Faith signifies perfect and complete trust in Christ. When we walk closely to Him, fiery darts have no power. We quickly apply what we believe, always pointing to God's Word, His character, His unfailing love, and His promises, knowing He is always true and faithful. By using our shield of faith, we depend on God and His grace in Christ. We link ourselves in mind and thought to God who has all power and will enable us to be "more than conquerors" (Romans 8:37).

6. What "dart" comes to your mind and causes confusion most often?

7. What Scripture verses can you use to counteract it?

Helmet of Salvation

The Roman soldier's helmet, called a galea, was required for battle. A cap made of leather strengthened by plates of metal gave it a protective quality.

"'You are my witnesses,' declares the LORD, 'and my servant whom I have chosen, so that you may know and believe me and understand that I am he.'"

—Isaiah 43:10

The apostle Paul wrote of the helmet of salvation, drawing attention to the Christian's mind, brain, understanding, and thinking. Throughout Scripture, Jesus warned His followers that they would have great trials and tribulations. Satan attacks us through our thought life with lies, weariness, persecution, temptation, unjust criticism, and unfair judgments. Words come that wound our spirits and can cripple our faith if we take them personally. We see the seemingly happy and prosperous unbelieving families around us and are tempted to feel we have lived a righteous life for no purpose. The heartbreak of our loved one's sexual brokenness discourages us and tempts us to think, *It's no use. I try to live a godly life, and look what happens.*

Romans 12:2 reminds us that we are not to be conformed to the world's desires but to "be transformed by the renewing of your mind." Our minds are open playgrounds for Satan's deceptions. What we believe impacts our relationships, our decisions, and our behavior. We continually interpret life on both a conscious and subconscious level because of deeply held, internalized beliefs. If we do not "inform" those thoughts and impact them with the fresh perspective of God's truth, we are living in our own darkness.

8. How has your study of God's Word impacted your thoughts? Give one example.

9. What verse can you stand on to protect your mind and give you the hope of eternal life?

Sword of the Spirit

The Roman soldier tucked his sword under his belt for easy access. The sword represents God's Word that we daily put into our minds and reinforce with memorization. We are not to fight the devil with our own power or human rationalization, but with God's Word. The Holy Spirit also gives us understanding of the Word and guides us in the proper use of it, so when we come up against the tough issues, we can respond out of God's strength and be effective. An example is found in Matthew 4:1-11 where Jesus quoted Scripture in response to Satan's temptations.

Note Jesus' first words in response to Satan: "It is written: 'Man shall not live on bread alone, but on every word that comes from the mouth of God'" (v. 4).

10. Give an example of how God's Word has helped you fight Satan in the past or how it could combat temptation for you today.

> "Prayer is the slender nerve that moves the muscle of omnipotence."
> —Charles Spurgeon

Prayer

After the apostle Paul described each piece of armor, he emphasized our most powerful weapon: prayer. "And pray in the Spirit on all occasions with all kinds of prayers and requests. With this in mind, be alert and always keep on praying for all the Lord's people" (Ephesians 6:18). Constant communication with God allows the armor of God to be effective and gives us access to His power, which is always available to us. Remember, Nehemiah's strength came from his sincere dependence on God and his life of prayer.

Prayer is essential to the Christian life, and it is a discipline that can be learned. Even the disciples asked Jesus how to pray after they observed how fervent and personal His prayer life with the Father was. Jesus' answer was the Lord's Prayer, which many of us have memorized.

Prayers vary from personal petitions to prewritten supplications. Great prayers reflect a heart committed to Jesus, a fervency of spirit, and a faith that believes in the power of prayer. Praying God's Word is a powerful way to pray in faith. As you learn to pray, your prayer life grows stronger.

Praying in the Spirit means the Holy Spirit directs the prayer process, creates the prayer within us, and empowers us to pray it. "We do not know what we ought to pray for, but the Spirit himself intercedes for us through wordless groans. And he who searches our hearts knows the mind of the Spirit, because the Spirit intercedes for God's people in accordance with the will of God" (Romans 8:26-27). How precious to know that the Holy Spirit loves us so much He takes our wordless, agonized hearts and intercedes at God's throne for us!

Applying the Armor

As we begin to understand God's armor, He can show us how to apply it to our lives. The following personal illustration may help.

"You will keep in perfect peace those whose minds are steadfast, because they trust in you."
—Isaiah 26:3

One evening while serving in ministry, I received an avalanche of abusive, personal attacks from a friend. At the time, I was preparing a lesson for Sunday school; and the accusations left me vulnerable and heartbroken. I fled to a private place and cried until no more tears came. I complained to God about my situation and questioned whether I could even teach the next day.

After I pulled myself together, I reread the lesson. It was taken from 2 Samuel 24, the story of King David's disobedience to God's instruction about counting the troops. When David realized what he had done, he was conscience-stricken. Gad, a prophet of God, instructed David to build an altar to the Lord on the threshing floor of Araunah, the Jebusite, in order to stop the consequences of David's disobedience.

David attempted to buy the land from Araunah. However, Araunah told David the land, as well as the wood and oxen for the sacrifice, didn't need to be purchased because David was the king. David responded, "No, I insist on paying you for it. I will not sacrifice to the LORD my God burnt offerings that cost me nothing" (v. 24).

God took David's words and applied them to my heart. "Are you willing to sacrifice your hurt and pain to me? Doing so will cost you. You will need to give up feeling sorry for yourself and forgive."

God's words resonated in my heart, but I didn't know how to proceed. I prayed, "Lord, show me how to sacrifice my hurt and pain to You."

God reminded me, "'It is mine to avenge; I will repay'" (Romans 12:19). I knew from my studies that harboring unforgiveness and hurt in my heart was giving Satan an open door to my life. Forgiving and letting go was a conscious choice I had to make. I had to take off my outer garments of pride and self-centeredness and humble myself before Him. "Oh, Lord, forgive me," I cried. "I choose You. I give You my pain and my hurt, and I trust You to handle them. My situation is in Your hands."

God gave me incredible peace as I turned my feelings over to Him. The process became a pattern whenever someone hurt me. I was honest with God about my pain; and after grieving, I sacrificed it to Him.

Out of that experience, God gave me a picture in my mind of a soldier in armor, and I was inside that armor being protected by Him. Applying God's armor is sacrificing our understanding, our pride, our truth, our pain, our loved one—whatever God points out to us—and making a conscious decision to give whatever it is back to Him.

When we turn and fully commit ourselves into God's hands, we can begin to praise Him for His answers—for taking care of our loved ones, for bringing peace and wholeness into our homes and lives. Giving praise and thanks to God is the essence of faith itself. "Those who sacrifice thank offerings honor me, and to the blameless I will show my salvation" (Psalm 50:23).

11. List the things you can praise God for up to this time.

> "Let us hold unswervingly to the hope we profess, for he who promised is faithful."
> —Hebrews 10:23

12. In faith, list what you anticipate praising Him for in the future.

Persevering

Nehemiah never gave up. With each new problem that arose, he prayed and continued building. The odds were against him, but he remained in the fight until the walls were built. Miraculously, they were built in fifty-two days.

Nehemiah's enemies were overcome: "When all our enemies heard about this, all the surrounding nations were afraid and lost their self-confidence, because they realized that this work had been done with the help of our God" (Nehemiah 6:16).

Sexual brokenness is not an equal-rights issue or a harmless behavior. It is Satan's scheme against God's plan for humanity and his way of destroying individuals and families. The entrapment of sexual brokenness cannot be fought without God. Satan's influence in our lives and in the lives of our loved ones is cunning and shrewd, but we can partner with God for their salvation and transformation. Turning our loved ones over to God, waiting on Him, and trusting in Him is the key.

"If we are to pray aright, perhaps it is quite necessary that we pray contrary to our own heart. Not what we want to pray is important, but what God wants us to pray.... The richness of the Word of God ought to determine our prayer, not the poverty of our heart."

—Dietrich Bonhoeffer

REBUILDING

When you become a soldier, you are sworn in. No battle can be fought with half-hearted interest. Soldiers pledge to be faithful and fight for the cause. God asks no less of us. No matter what our circumstances, we must remain fully committed to God's will and way in our lives.

In order to win the battle, we need to be clothed in God's armor at all times. Which piece of this armor is most difficult for you to apply to your life?

What can you do to make putting it on easier?

Memorize Ephesians 6:10-18.

Then ask the Holy Spirit to guide you as you create a prayer for yourself that spells out applying the armor of God. If you don't know where to start, you can use the following prayer as a guide. (Note that quotes from and adaptations of Scripture make up the body of this prayer. Praying God's Word is a powerful way to pray.)

Dear Lord Jesus,

Thank you for being my Savior and Lord. "You are a compassionate and gracious God, slow to anger and abounding in love and faithfulness" (Psalm 86:15). Hear my prayer, dear Lord, and listen to my cries for mercy (Psalm 86:6-7). I confess that I am full of pride—that I flatter myself too much to detect or hate my sin (Psalm 36:2). Please forgive me and "create in me a pure heart, O God, and renew a steadfast spirit within me" (Psalm 51:10). I submit myself to You and Your will for my life.

I put on the full armor of God as You commanded me through the apostle Paul (Ephesians 6:13). I understand that I can do nothing unless I remain in You and You in me (John

15:4). All my "righteous acts are like filthy rags" (Isaiah 64:6). Make me strong in You and in Your mighty power (Ephesians 6:10). Thank You for making Jesus to be sin for me, so in him I might become Your righteousness (2 Corinthians 5:21). Sanctify me "by the truth; your Word is truth" (John 17:17). "Guide me in your truth and teach me, for you are God, my Savior" (Psalm 25:5). Help me to submit to Your righteousness in my life, not my own (Romans 10:3).

Thank You for Your peace that is a gift of my salvation. Your peace guards my heart and mind in Christ Jesus (Philippians 4:7). "Give me an undivided heart, that I may fear your name" (Psalm 86:11). Fix Your words in my heart and mind (Deuteronomy 11:18). Open my mind, so I may understand the Scriptures (Luke 24:45). Transform me by the renewing of my mind, so I will be able to test and approve what Your good and perfect will is (Romans 12:2). Protect my mind from the god of this age (2 Corinthians 4:4).

Fill me with Your Holy Spirit, Lord, so I may speak Your Word boldly (Acts 4:31). Fill me with Your joy (Acts 13:52). May I "overflow with hope by the power of the Holy Spirit" (Romans 15:13). I delight in You, Lord. Let Your ear be attentive to my prayer (Nehemiah 1:11). I have set my mind to gain understanding and humble myself before You (Daniel 10:12).

Lord, I love You with all my heart, all my soul, all my mind, and all my strength (Mark 12:30). Teach me how to love You more each day, be attentive to Your voice, and hold fast to You (Deuteronomy 30:20).

I present this prayer and petition with thanksgiving (Philippians 4:6). "Praise and glory and wisdom and thanks and honor and power and strength" be to You, my God, forever and ever. Amen (Revelation 7:12).

CONTINUING YOUR JOURNEY

The walls of Jerusalem rose from heaps of rubble under God's mighty hand in fifty-two days—a true miracle! How could this happen? Who was this man, Nehemiah? How could a humble cupbearer, an alien slave to King Artaxerxes, the son of Babylonian refugees, lead this incredible effort? Because one man dreamed and believed God could make a difference through him, rebuilt walls emerged. Nehemiah submitted his heart's desires to God, prayed for God's leading, and took action to achieve what God laid on his heart to do.

Nehemiah's accomplishment did not derive from his excellent plans, his great relationship with the king, or his construction skills. He succeeded because he wholly believed in God, depended on Him, and allowed God to use him. Along the way, Nehemiah encountered opposition but remained faithful to God's call.

If you keep reading the book of Nehemiah, you will notice his problems did not end with rebuilding the walls. God continued to use him to bring the Israelites back to faith in God, to become all God wanted them to be. Reclaiming, restoring, and rebuilding the hearts of the Jewish people demanded years of Nehemiah's life and leadership.

Healing sexual brokenness draws on our commitment to faith, endurance, and dependence on God. Like Nehemiah, challenges strengthen us and bring us new resolve. Even if our family members decide to walk away from same-sex behavior or transgenderism and commit or recommit their lives to the Lord, becoming who God desires them to be is not an overnight phenomenon. The damage that gave fertile soil to the development of sexual brokenness must be plowed and reseeded. Temptations to go back into homosexual behavior or a transgendered life will be encountered. Strong cultural influences will affirm their broken sexuality, and you will be targeted as an object of taunting and derision. Are you ready for this adventure with God?

Whether our loved ones come out of sexual brokenness or remain in it, our ongoing challenge will be to love them unconditionally while standing firm in the authority of God's Word. To manage this delicate balance successfully, we will be forced to grow in our prayer lives, live daily in the truth of His Word, and depend on the Holy Spirit to lead us through the tough times.

If we let God do His work in us, we will someday be able to look back on our experience and say with the Psalmist, "It was good for me to be afflicted so that I might learn your decrees. The law from your mouth is more precious to me than thousands of pieces of silver and gold" (Psalm 119:71-72).

A Prayer for You

"When I think of the wisdom and scope of his plan, I fall down on my knees and pray to the Father of all the great family of God—some of them already in heaven and some down here on earth—that out of his glorious, unlimited resources he will give you the mighty inner strengthening of his Holy Spirit.

"And I pray that Christ will be more and more at home in your hearts, living within you as you trust in him. May your roots go down deep into the soil of God's marvelous love; and may you be able to feel and understand, as all God's children should, how long, how wide, how deep, and how high his love really is; and to experience this love for yourselves, though it is so great that you will never see the end of it or fully know or understand it. And so at last you will be filled up with God himself.

"Now glory be to God, who by his mighty power at work within us is able to do far more than we would ever dare to ask or even dream of—infinitely beyond our highest prayers, desires, thoughts, or hopes. May he be given glory forever and ever through endless ages because of his master plan of salvation for the Church through Jesus Christ" (Ephesians 3:14-21 TLB).

RECOMMENDED READING

Homosexuality

Allender, Dan B., *The Wounded Heart: Hope for Adult Victims of Childhood Sexual Abuse*. Colorado Springs, CO: NavPress, 1990.

Sexual abuse is a major contributor to sexual brokenness, and Allender gives insights into the results of abuse and God's path to healing.

Barr, Adam T., and Ron Citlau, *Compassion Without Compromise: How the Gospel Frees Us to Love Our Gay Friends Without Losing the Truth*. Bloomington, MN: Bethany House Publishers, 2014.

Two pastors offer compassionate, biblical answers to homosexuality and practical, real-world advice on how to think and talk about this controversial issue with loved ones.

Black, Stephen H., *Freedom Realized: Finding Freedom from Homosexuality and Living a Life Free from Labels*. Enumclaw, WA: Redemption Press, 2017.

This book contains Black's story of redemption from homosexuality, as well as insights from sixteen seasoned ex-gay leaders for overcoming same-sex attractions.

Boynes, Janet, *Called Out: A Former Lesbian's Discovery of Freedom*. Lake Mary, FL: Creation House, 2008.

Boynes tell the story of her walk to freedom out of a lesbian lifestyle.

Boynes, Janet, *God & Sexuality: Truth and Relevance Without Compromise*. Tulsa, OK: Harrison House Publishers, 2016.

Boynes speaks with candor to people who question God's truth regarding homosexuality. This is a good book for pastors and church leaders.

Brown, Michael L., *Can You Be Gay and Christian?* Lake Mary, FL: Frontline, 2014.

Brown tackles the tough questions about "gay Christians" with compassion and solid biblical answers.

Cloud, Henry, and John Townsend, *Boundaries: When to Say Yes, How to Say No to Take Control of Your Life*. Grand Rapids, MI: Zondervan, 1992.

Cloud and Townsend give biblically based answers to tough questions about setting healthy boundaries with family members, friends, coworkers, and even ourselves. This book is especially helpful when needing to set boundaries with sexually broken family members.

Comiskey, Andrew, *Pursuing Sexual Wholeness*. Lake Mary, FL: Siloam, 1989.

Comiskey, founder of Desert Stream Ministries, provides biblical and practical answers for overcoming homosexuality.

Dallas, Joe, *Desires in Conflict*, revised. Eugene, OR: Harvest House Publishers, 2003.

Dallas writes directly to the Christian who struggles with homosexual temptations. This book is a great resource for family and friends who wish to understand the complexities of same-sex attractions.

Dallas, Joe, *The Gay Gospel?* Eugene, OR: Harvest House Publishers, 2007.

From a personal perspective, Dallas gives a detailed understanding of pro-gay theology and a clear, biblical response.

Dallas, Joe, *Speaking of Homosexuality: Discussing the Issues with Kindness and Clarity*. Grand Rapids, MI: Baker Books, 2016.

Dallas reviews arguments in favor of normalizing homosexuality and helps readers understand the views of LGBT people and how to respond with clarity, confidence, and compassion.

Dallas, Joe, *When Homosexuality Hits Home*. Eugene, OR: Harvest House Publishers, 2015.

This practical book deals with homosexuality in the family and answers common questions posed by family members.

Dallas, Joe, and Nancy Heche, eds., *The Complete Christian Guide to Understanding Homosexuality*. Eugene, OR: Harvest House Publishers, 2010.

This book is an authoritative and comprehensive guide to homosexuality from a Christian perspective.

Groom, Nancy, *From Bondage to Bonding: Escaping Codependency, Embracing Biblical Love*. Colorado Springs, CO: NavPress, 1991.

Groom addresses the issue of emotional dependency in relationships, which is especially helpful for sexual addicts and spouses of the sexually broken.

Haley, Mike, *101 Frequently Asked Questions about Homosexuality*. Eugene, OR: Harvest House Publishers, 2004.

Answers to questions about homosexuality, fielded by a former homosexual who is an expert on the subject.

Hallman, Janelle, *The Heart of Female Same-Sex Attraction: A Comprehensive Counseling Resource*. Downers Grove, IL: InterVarsity Press, 2008.

Hallman has specialized in working with same-sex-attracted women for many years, and her insights and understanding are beneficial for both parents and counselors.

Heche, Nancy, *The Truth Comes Out*. Ventura, CA: Regal Books, 2006.

Drawing from her personal experiences as a wife and mother, Heche speaks of the transformation of her heart regarding homosexuality.

Moberly, Elizabeth R., *Homosexuality: A New Christian Ethic*. Cambridge, UK: Lutterworth Press, 2006.

A research psychologist, formerly at Cambridge University, presents a theory of homosexual root causes.

Nicolosi, Joseph, and Linda Ames Nicolosi, *A Parent's Guide to Preventing Homosexuality*. Downers Grove, IL: InterVarsity Press, 2002.

This book is an excellent guide to understanding and developing healthy gender identity in children.

Paulk, Anne, *Restoring Sexual Identity*. Eugene, OR: Harvest House Publishers, 2003.

Paulk offers answers to the difficult and often heart-wrenching questions that women with same-sex attractions ask.

Payne, Leanne, *The Broken Image: Restoring Personal Wholeness through Healing Prayer*. Grand Rapids, MI: Baker Books, 1995.

Payne exposes the power of healing prayer reaching deep wounds at the heart of homosexuality.

Payne, Leanne, *Crisis in Masculinity*. Grand Rapids, MI: Baker Books, 1995.

Payne delves into the depths of manhood, showing that, with God's healing power, masculinity can be developed in any man at any age.

Takle, David, *The Truth About Lies and Lies About Truth,* revised. High Point, NC: Kingdom Formation Ministries, 2017.

A proper understanding of belief, truth, and deception are essential for Christian growth and recovery and necessary for dealing with the cause and effects of sin. This book is excellent for further understanding the reasons behind sexual brokenness.

White, John, *Parents in Pain: Overcoming the Hurt and Frustration of Problem Children*. Downers Grove, IL: InterVarsity Press, 1979.

Many parents face problems beyond their ability to cope. White offers comfort to parents of children with tough problems like alcoholism, homosexuality, and suicide.

Worthen, Anita, and Bob Davies, *Someone I Love Is Gay: How Family and Friends Can Respond*. Downers Grove, IL: InterVarsity Press, 1996.

The authors offer easy-to-understand answers and real-life examples for family members.

Yuan, Christopher, and Angela Yuan, *Out of a Far Country: A Gay Son's Journey to God, A Broken Mother's Search for Hope*. Colorado Springs, CO: WaterBrook Press, 2011.

This amazing, real-life story offers hope to families impacted by homosexuality.

Transgenderism

Heyer, Walt, *Gender Lies and Suicide*. CreateSpace, 2013.

Heyer analyzes issues that fuel transgender suicide and shares stories from people who seek to undo their decision to change genders.

Heyer, Walt, *Paper Genders: Pulling the Mask Off the Transgender Phenomenon*. Carlsbad, CA: Make Waves Publishing, 2011.

Heyer debunks the glowing promises of gender change and exposes the truth transgender advocates want to keep hidden.

Heyer, Walt, *A Transgender's Faith*. CreateSpace, 2015.

Heyer tells one man's powerful testimony of his restoration to his birth gender.

Shick, Denise, ed., *Dangerous Affirmations: "Should I Have Been Daddy's Little Girl?"* Ashland, KY: Help 4 Families, 2014.

Shick tells the personal story of a young boy who struggles to live in his male gender.

Shick, Denise, *Transgender Confusion: A Biblical Based Q and A for Families*. CreateSpace, 2016.

This book offers a look at real-life situations endured by families facing transgender issues and what can be done to help them.

Shick, Denise, *Understanding Gender Confusion: A Faith Based Perspective*. CreateSpace, 2014.

Shick discusses the issues behind gender confusion and why restoration does not happen overnight.

Shick, Denise, *When Hope Seems Lost*. Ashland, KY: Help4Familes Press, 2015.

This helpful resource for churches and families facing issues of gender confusion uses a combination of insights and real-life stories.

Shick, Denise, and Jerry Gramckow, *My Daddy's Secret*, CreateSpace, 2015.

The authors tell the true story of the effects of a father's secret sexual addictions on his family, along with insights into the pain inflicted on families.

STAGES OF GRIEF
FOR FAMILIES IMPACTED
BY SEXUAL BROKENNESS

Family members experience grief in various stages, although not necessarily in the order presented here. Some may skip a stage; others may recycle through the stages more than once.

Shock/Denial

Family members' responses to their loved one's same-sex attractions or gender preference vary. Sometimes the news comes from the affected individual, other times through family members or friends. Facing the magnitude of the truth they have been told causes shock, numbness, or disbelief. Refusing to accept the news may last for a few days or months.

Emotional Release

When the coming-out of the loved one becomes real, family members may react with strong emotions, such as yelling, screaming, or crying. Physical reactions, such as putting a fist through a wall, can also occur.

Depression, Loneliness, and Utter Isolation

Because shame and disgrace surround sexual brokenness, family members hold the news inside, withdraw from normal relationships, and question whom they might trust with the truth. A sense that no one understands or cares brings about depression, loneliness, isolation, and feelings of hopelessness.

Physical Symptoms of Distress

As the mind and heart acknowledge grief and emotional distress, the body begins to show signs of physical illness with symptoms related to loss. These physical signs include insomnia, nightmares, diet changes, drug abuse, alcohol use, and uncontrolled weeping.

Panic

Unable to think properly and emotionally overwhelmed by stress, family members begin to panic and question their sanity. Unable to cope, individuals think they might be losing their minds.

Guilt

A loved one's coming-out causes other family members to recall past situations of abuse, neglect, or mistreatment of that person. A family member's guilt may feel especially acute if he or she had any part in what happened to the loved one. Parents, in particular, will go back through the entire lifetime of a son or daughter, looking for incidents that might or did cause sexual or gender confusion or for other people who are perceived to be responsible. The guilt may be imaginary or real. Regret turns into "if onlys" of what should have, could have, might have happened if they had done the right thing.

Hostility

Grief over the situation, disruption in the family, and a level of frustration over why sexual brokenness had to happen turns into overwhelming anger toward the loved one who caused the upheaval.

Inability to Renew Normal Activities

Shock and grief occur in the family, and processing takes time. Family members, as well as affected loved ones, try to make sense of what happened. Getting back to business-as-usual is difficult and includes struggling to concentrate, feeling disorganized, and avoiding normal relationships.

Bargaining

In an attempt to change behavior or lifestyle, family members bargain with loved ones or God to achieve a different outcome. Money, gifts, promises to attend church, etc., all become part of the bargaining process.

Gradually Overcoming Grief

While the sense of loss to the family never totally goes away, the emotional swings slow down and wounds begin to heal.

Readjustment to New Reality

As family members move through the above stages and face reality, grief dissipates, compassion for others surfaces, and stronger and better people emerge.

PRAYERS FOR PRODIGALS

These Scripture-based prayers are designed to be prayed for any loved one (son, daughter, grandchild, child of a friend, spouse, or parent) who has strayed from God into a destructive lifestyle. For the sake of clarity, the prayers are written with a son in mind; but adapt them to your situation. Also read the Bible passages associated with each prayer.

Lord, protect my son. Build a hedge around him to guard him physically, emotionally, and spiritually. Block his paths, so he cannot move toward activities and relationships that would harm him. *(Job 1:10; Hosea 2:6-7)*

Deliver him from evil. Rescue him from a destructive lifestyle. Restore him to his senses, and bring him home from the land of the enemy. *(Matthew 6:13; Psalm 91:14; Luke 15:17; Jeremiah 31:16-17)*

Guide my son into the truth. Teach him to recognize deceptive ideas and thoughts. Make him alert to the lies of the enemy, and teach him how to resist the devil by faith. *(John 16:13; Colossians 2:8; 1 Peter 5:8-9)*

Give my son the courage to be honest with himself and with You. Spirit of God, convict him of sin and his need for You. Don't allow my son to blame others for troubles in his life. Show him that he alone is responsible for his choices. *(John 16:8; Genesis 3:12-13; Ezekiel 18:20)*

Lord, thank You for drawing my son with love and tenderness to Yourself, even in his desert place. Show him You are with him. You delight in him. Amid the clamor for his attention and affections, may he hear Your voice calling him and respond to Your deep, deep love. *(Jeremiah 31:13; Hosea 2:14; Zephaniah 3:17)*

Cause my son to call out to You in his distress and confusion. Cause him to seek You with abandon. Thank You for promising to answer him. *(Psalm 91:15; Jeremiah 29:13)*

Remove my son's heart of stone; and replace it with a new, soft heart. Make this heart into a bed of fertile soil, so the seed of truth sown into it will grow deep roots and bring forth a rich crop of life. *(Ezekiel 36:26-27; Matthew 13:23; Colossians 2:6-7)*

Lord Jesus, reveal to my son that lasting refreshment and satisfaction can only be found in You. In You he will find an abundant life. *(John 4:10; 10:10; Psalm 1:3)*

Lead my son to friends who will graciously point him to You. Cause him to be attracted to those who are attracted to You. Scatter like chaff in the wind any friends who will bring him harm. Give him the courage to please You, not man. *(Proverbs 13:20; Galatians 1:10)*

Produce in my son a humble spirit that is yielded to You. Teach him how to live in You; and show him that apart from You, he can do nothing. *(James 4:10; Romans 6:13; John 15:5)*

Teach my son to live in freedom, animated and motivated by Your spirit and in step with Him. *(Galatians 5:16, 25)*

—*B. J. Reinhard*

SEXUAL BROKENNESS: A BIBLICAL PERSPECTIVE

The following treatise presents an overview of scriptures taken from my day-to-day reading of God's Word over a period of years. Hopefully, these ideas not only give you a general understanding of God's desire for a relationship with Him, but also how these principles apply to sexual brokenness and His plans for humanity.

In the context of this study, sexual brokenness focuses primarily on homosexuality and transgenderism. Related behaviors, such as sexual abuse, use of pornography, adultery, fornication, incest, bisexuality, pedophilia, and bestiality, are not directly covered but play a role in the overall spectrum of sexual brokenness.

As I write this section, I am aware of the emotional and psychological anguish experienced by people who identify as gay, lesbian, homosexual, or transgender. My heart (and God's heart) grieves for people who have experienced abuse and rejection on their life's journey. It is important to remember that these individuals have not chosen their unfortunate surroundings and, therefore, find it difficult to understand why they are responsible to implement changes in their lives.

At the same time, we choose what we believe. How we implement these beliefs determines how we live here on Earth and where we will spend eternity. The lie we often believe is that we can fix ourselves—we don't need anyone. Speaking truth from God's perspective is necessary to understand what He requires for wholeness. He is a holy God and cannot abide the presence of sin. He does not bow to our self-pity and selfishness but holds us responsible for the way we respond to the temptations that come our way, as well as evil perpetrated against us. He is a God of mercy and grace, as well as a God of truth. When we humble ourselves before Him, turning away from our sin, He is willing and able to forgive our sins and restore us to Himself.

God created us in His image.

"In the beginning, God" (Genesis 1:1). What beautiful words express the opening narrative of the Bible, God's letter to mankind! How comforting and precious to know God as an ever-present reality, both now and for millions of people throughout the ages. God exists; He always existed; and He always will exist. Everything begins and ends with God: "'I am the Alpha and the Omega,' says the Lord God, 'who is, and who was, and who is to come, the Almighty'" (Revelation 1:8).

God is a person, a spiritual being. His creative acts portray our first glimpse of who He is. Out of a formless mass, He created order and symmetry. God called forth light first because it makes life possible and His creative works visible. "'I am the LORD, and there is no other. I form the light and create darkness'" (Isaiah 45:6-7).

Step by step, day after day, God's words "Let there be" continued to form the heavens and the earth, the seas and dry ground, living creatures, the sun and moon, insects and plants. His incredible handiwork and exceptional artistry reflect the beauty of our world today. "And God saw that it was good" (Genesis 1:12).

In Genesis 1:20, the creation story changed slightly from God forming the heavens and the earth to creating living creatures, the birds of the air and creatures of the sea. His blessing allowed all living things to flourish, reproduce themselves, and fill the earth with life. He then announced His crowning work, human beings, whom He would make in His image. Men and women were the climax of God's creative activity, and God "crowned them with glory and honor" (Psalm 8:5), delegating them to rule over the rest of creation. As such, every human being is worthy of honor and respect. "So God created mankind in his own image, in the image of God he created Him; male and female he created them" (Genesis 1:27).

What was it about God's image that made humanity different from every other living animal? God's distinctive imprint identified people as His special creation, which meant they had characteristics that no other living creature would have. Human beings duplicate God's spiritual/moral nature, giving them the ability to be in relationship with Him, comprehend His ways, love Him, and commune with Him.

God bestowed on humanity the capacity to relate to other humans, think, deliberate, reason, reflect, and grow. He gifted men and women with memory; intellect; moral discernment; and, ultimately, the ability to make decisions, to choose. With this gift of choice, people can choose to serve God or go their own way. God blessed His special creation with these words: "'Be fruitful and increase in number; fill the earth and subdue it. Rule over the fish in the sea and the birds in the sky and over every living creature that moves on the ground'" (Genesis 1:28).

God made human beings in His image. Among the other characteristics already mentioned, humans are spiritual beings. God's gift to us—and His plan for us—is to be immortal, to be in relationship with Him eternally. The note on Ecclesiastes 3:11 in the *NIV Study Bible* says it well: "Since we were made for eternity, the things of time cannot fully and permanently satisfy" (Kenneth Barker, ed., Grand Rapids, MI: Zondervan Publishing House, 1995, p. 1290).

God gave us boundaries for our sexual behavior.

God's love for us is unconditional. Yet, like a good parent, God puts boundaries in place to safeguard His human creation. Boundaries allow for independence but also limit the sphere of behaviors that are acceptable to Him. If we choose to love and follow God, we voluntarily decide to accept His terms and boundaries and to abide by them. These boundaries are motivated by His love for us and provide the security of His protection. His Word makes clear the precepts He desires us to keep.

Our greatest joy will come from loving God and living lives of obedience to Him.

Two of God's greatest commandments are: "'Love the Lord your God with all your heart and with all your soul and with all your strength and with all your mind'; and, 'Love your neighbor as yourself'" (Luke 10:27; see also Romans 13:8-10; Matthew 22:37-39; Mark 12:29-33; and Galatians 5:13-20). Love for God is linked to our obedience to Him, and love for God is exemplified by our obedience to His precepts (1 John 5:1-3; 2 John 6; John 14:15, 21-23; 15:9-10; Romans 2:13).

Only two sexual intimacy options are biblically accepted: marriage or celibacy.

Immoral sexual behavior—both heterosexual and homosexual—is considered idolatry in Scripture, as it takes the place of God in our lives (Ephesians 5:5; Colossians 3:5). Over and over, God condemns idolatry, the worship of gods other than Himself. This fact is specifically spelled out in the second commandment of the Ten Commandments: "'You shall have no other gods before me'" (Exodus 20:3; Deuteronomy 5:7).

When it comes to human sexuality, immoral sexual behavior rejects God's will for men and women, placing personal pleasure ahead of God's desires for human lives. Using another human being to fulfill one's sexual needs outside a commitment to marriage amounts to sinning against that person.

Heterosexual, monogamous marriage is the fulfillment of God's creative order.

God created the institution of marriage (Genesis 2:22-24; Matthew 19:3-9) and has the right to define its boundaries and restrictions. The holy union of marriage is designed to be between one genetically defined man (born biologically male at birth) and one genetically defined woman (born biologically female at birth). Jesus also limited the sexual union to two persons, male and female. Any other pairing deviates from God's stated boundaries for marriage.

God created male and female for the purposes of procreation and companionship (Genesis 1:26-28; 2:18-24). God's full image comes together in the marriage union of male and female and is an earthly portrayal of God's holy union with His people (Ephesians 5:22-23). Marriage is not to be entered into casually or lightly. The institution of marriage is one of the building blocks of a healthy society, and God designed it to be exclusive. Any sexual experiences outside the one-man, one-woman marital bond are against His created order (Genesis 2:22-24; Matthew 19:3-9). Affirming homosexual or transgender marriages is an active negation of God's will for humanity and an active rebellion against the creation of sexual differentiation.

The Bible is clear in its position on homosexuality.

Same-sex sexual behavior, homosexuality, is mentioned explicitly in the following scriptures: Leviticus 18:22; 20:13; Romans 1:26-27; 1 Corinthians 6:9-10; Jude 7. It is spoken of as being displeasing to God and prohibited. Two additional stories, Lot and the men of Sodom in Genesis 19:4-11 and the story of rape in Judges 19:22-25, also condemn the practice of homosexuality.

Whenever Scripture addresses homosexuality, it does not condemn the *person* but condemns the *behavior*, which includes one's active and deliberate thought life. The temptation or impassive experience of unwanted sexual desires does not bring condemnation. (For further reading, see *The Gay Gospel?* by Joe Dallas.)

God also has views on transgenderism.

Looking at God's creation, it is easy to see His perfection regarding genders. God created both men and women intentionally with special characteristics and distinctions exclusive to that gender. He declared both male and female "very good" (Genesis 1:27, 31). Deuteronomy 22:5 and 1 Corinthians 6:9 indicate God's displeasure with blurring the distinction between the sexes. Crossing the gender boundary (attempting to switch genders), tempting as it may be for some people, implies that God made an error in the gender assignment. God does not make mistakes in His creation (Deuteronomy 32:3-4; Matthew 5:48; 1 John 1:5). "He is the Maker of all things, . . . the LORD Almighty is his name" (Jeremiah 10:16).

God designed us to bring glory to Him.

Same-sex sexual behavior, immoral heterosexual sexual behavior, and changing one's God-given gender do not bring glory to God. These are all manifestations of the worship of self.

Glory is defined in the Old Testament through the Hebrew word *kabod*, which means "weight, importance, radiance" (Richard S. Taylor, ed., *Beacon Dictionary of Theology*, Kansas City, MO: Beacon Hill Press, 1983, p. 234). We are to reflect in our person and life the importance and radiance of God, as well as His holiness. God created us to bring glory to Himself (Isaiah 43:7). We are to "do it all for the glory of God" (1 Corinthians 10:31). Sexual sin signals a change in thinking. "Although they claimed to be wise, they became fools and exchanged the glory of the immortal God for images made to look like a mortal human being" (Romans 1:21-23).

As Christians, we are to live holy lives, lives "set apart" from the world.

God commanded us to "be holy, because I, the LORD your God, am holy" (Leviticus 19:1-2; see also Leviticus 20:7-8, 26; Isaiah 62:12; 1 Corinthians 3:17; 6:19; Ephesians 1:4; 1 Peter

1:16). Holiness is the essence of God's character. When we choose to serve God, we choose to partake of His holiness. "It is His holiness that in love necessitated the Cross. It is His holiness that likewise necessitates the ultimate separation of the holy and the unholy (Rev. 22:11, 15)" (Richard S. Taylor, ed., *Beacon Dictionary of Theology*, Kansas City, MO: Beacon Hill Press, 1983, p. 259).

Sexual immorality and gender reassignment surgery is inconsistent with God's instruction that we live holy lives (Hebrews 12:14; also 2 Corinthians 7:1; Ephesians 5:3; 1 Thessalonians 4:3-8; 1 Peter 1:13-15; Mark 7:21; and Romans 6:19).

Our bodies are "God's temple."

As the apostle Paul wrote in 1 Corinthians 3:17, "If anyone destroys God's temple, God will destroy that person; for God's temple is sacred, and you together are that temple." Our bodies were not designed for sexual immorality. When we participate in same-sex sexual behaviors or immoral heterosexual sexual behaviors, we sin against our bodies (1 Corinthians 6:18). Homosexual behavior involves practices that are injurious to the body and involve a high risk of infectious disease, even apart from HIV/AIDS.

Choosing to change to the opposite gender is defiling the temple God created us to be.

Sexual immorality inhibits spiritual maturity.

What does it mean to work out our salvation? How do we grow and mature spiritually if we continue to go against God's will? (See Philippians 2:12; 1 Timothy 4:7-8; Luke 9:23-25; 13:24; 14:33; John 12:23-26; James 4:7-10; Acts 24:16; and Romans 6:1; 12:1-2.) If we continue to live outside of God's plan and choose a life apart from Him, our hearts become hardened to our conscience and God's voice (Ephesians 4:18-20; Hebrews 12:16; Romans 8:5-8). Bitterness is often the result and destroys not only us but others around us. Eventually, due to our choices, we are slaves to our sin and lost to God.

God offers good news for the sexually broken.

Homosexuality and transgenderism are not hopeless! Sexual brokenness is not the unpardonable sin. Only one man ever lived a perfect life here on Earth: Jesus Christ.

God knows we are human and following the commands of a holy life are not easy. He loves us so much that He sent His one and only Son, Jesus, for the sole purpose of dying for our sins, so we might experience forgiveness and peace with Him (John 3:16). "God made him who had no sin to be sin for us, so that in him we might become the righteousness of God" (2 Corinthians 5:21).

Salvation is the gift God bestows on us as we come to Him in repentance. Turning away from our sin, humbling ourselves, and yielding to God are necessary for salvation, which doesn't end there. God also wants to restore our fallen nature and mold us into His image. He sends us the Holy Spirit to walk alongside us to lead and guide in our walks with Him. Complete surrender to the Lordship of Jesus Christ empowers the Holy Spirit to justify and sanctify us.

We will sin unintentionally. We will miss the mark. But when the Holy Spirit points out the things we need day-to-day to help us overcome our sins, we must follow them. Our faith is kept solid by humility, confession, and repentance. It is under the Holy Spirit's power that true healing begins "for it is God who works in you to will and to act in order to fulfill his good purpose" (Philippians 2:13).

In 1 Corinthians 6:9-11, sexual sins are spoken of as sins that are capable of being redeemed. Sexual sin, as well as other kinds of sin, are listed in this passage. Yet in verse 11, the apostle Paul wrote, "That is what some of you *were*" (emphasis added). When we repent of our sins and invite God into our hearts, we choose to obey Him and no longer choose to live out our sinful natures. If Scripture says these sins can be overcome—and it does—then change is possible. Change sometimes will mean eradication or diminishment of sinful desires but not always. When the desire remains, the Holy Spirit provides the power to resist those temptations.

In Romans 12:1 and 2, the apostle Paul tells us, "Therefore, I urge you, brothers and sisters, in view of God's mercy, to offer your bodies as a living sacrifice, holy and pleasing to God—this is your true and proper worship. Do not conform to the pattern of this world, but be transformed by the renewing of your mind. Then you will be able to test and approve what God's will is—his good, pleasing and perfect will."

Transforming our minds is foundational to healing. Reading and believing God's Word, participating in a Bible-believing church, praying, and thanking God for His answers transform our minds and hearts to conform to His will.

Change the ending.

Much of our culture is riddled by lies, and it is important to know the truth. People who believe embracing gender-identity labels is kind and loving or same-sex attraction is harmless promote distortion in the world and the church, leading many astray with false compassion. Proponents of "gay Christianity" legitimize and encourage continued bondage to lust, but God's grace is transformational. He makes a way of escape for those who are wholly committed to Him.

We must keep the doors open to our loved ones. Loving without approval keeps us walking in truth. Our loved ones may choose lives of sin and indulgence, but God will continue to work in them as we pray for them. Thank God regularly for His answers in advance, and praise Him for what you are learning in the process. Stand on God's promises; and be ready to welcome them home, encourage them, and do all you can to support their journeys out of sexual or gender confusion.

As a family member, pastor, or friend who wishes to help someone immersed in sexual brokenness, you would do well to read books from "Recommended Reading" on page 119 and seek help from ministries that have proven success in helping men and women come out of homosexuality and transgenderism. Many of these organizations are participating members of Restored Hope Network, www.restoredhopenetwork.org.

Finally, remember these words of C. S. Lewis: "You can't go back and change the beginning, but you can start where you are and change the ending."

LEADERS GUIDE

As you prepare to lead this study, read through the book of Nehemiah, asking God to show you insights that apply to your group members' journeys with homosexual or transgender loved ones. You may also find it helpful to read a commentary on this book for more information on Nehemiah's journey. *Be Determined* by Warren W. Wiersbe and *Ezra and Nehemiah* by J. Carl Laney are written for laypeople and are easy to understand.

Decide in advance if you want your group to be closed or open to new people. Once a group has started meeting together, members probably will feel more open with one another if new people are not added.

Guidelines for Facilitating Group Discussion

❏ Unless you have a large group, set the chairs in a circle to facilitate discussion.

❏ At the beginning of the first session, go around the circle and ask people to introduce themselves with an icebreaker question, such as hobby; favorite vacation place; favorite book, movie, or TV show; or favorite thing to do on Saturday.

❏ Explain that your group is a safe place for members to talk about their homosexual or transgender loved ones, the pain their choices have caused families, reactions to those choices, etc. Consider reading the following guidelines from Living Stones Ministries each week:

- We are gathered here to have a safe place to tell our stories, to learn more about homosexuality and transgenderism, to encourage one another, and to pray together.

- This group is open to whomever wishes to come, and it is meant to be a safe place where people can share authentic feelings. What we share here is intended to be confidential and stay in the group. Resist the temptation to share what you have heard here with others.

- Remember the sensitivity of others. Offensive language or explicit sexual details are not acceptable to this group.

- If you have something you think would be helpful or encouraging to another person, wait until that person finishes talking. Ask permission to share your thoughts. Using *I* words, you might say, for example, "When I had that situation in my family, I found that [name it] gave me renewed hope." Recognize that we cannot fix one another, and your "advice" may be offensive.

- If you wish to talk further following the meeting, you may stay to talk with other group members. However, please respect other people's time constraints.

❏ Encourage everyone to participate in the discussions, but don't force anyone to do so. Some people may be ready to talk from the beginning; others may sit silently for several sessions.

❏ Ask for volunteers to respond to questions, rather than calling on specific group members. At first, they may be hesitant to share their answers to personal questions until they get to know the others better. Rather than calling on anyone, give your response or move on to the next question.

❏ If you have a sexually broken loved one, participate in the discussions too. You are on this journey with group members, so come alongside them, rather than acting like you've solved your situation.

❏ Stay flexible. There may be times when it's more important to listen to someone share his or her story, respond appropriately, and pray for that person than to work through the questions. As you prepare to lead each session, ask for the Holy Spirit's guidance to know when to depart from the guide or stick with it.

Guidelines for Sessions

❏ This guide assumes each group member has a book and has worked through the questions before coming to the meetings. If not, read the Bible passages; discuss the questions together; complete or assign the "Rebuilding" activity; and assign the Bible verse memorization for the following meeting. For questions that may be too personal to share answers in a group, encourage everyone to answer them at home.

❏ You may want to start each session with a short worship time to focus attention on the God we seek to obey.

❏ Watch the time and adjust your questions accordingly. You may want to mark ones to skip if you need to. Allow enough time for the "Rebuilding" section and group prayer and still finish on time. Don't presume that group members will be okay with going longer. Some may, but others will need to leave.

❏ You may want to recommend a Bible translation to use for the verse memorization, so you can repeat it together in the group meeting.

❏ End each session with group prayer. Add variety by praying in different ways, such as breaking into smaller groups of two to four, calling for sentence prayers, or asking one or two volunteers to close.

1
Hearing the News

Purpose

To help group members realize they are not alone and God is working in their situations with sexually broken loved ones to bring about good.

Reflecting

Discuss the questions in this section.

Exploring

Question 1: Read the transition paragraph before the question, and have someone read Nehemiah 1:1-4. After one or more people answer this question, ask four volunteers to read about how other Bible characters responded to bad news:

- Esau: Genesis 27:41
- Naomi: Ruth 1:20-21
- Hannah: 1 Samuel 1:3-8
- Naaman: 2 Kings 5:11-12

  Then ask: Whose response most closely matches yours? Why?

Questions 2-13: Choose some or all of these questions to discuss together, using some of the text to introduce and tie them together. When a Bible passage is included, have one person read it aloud before asking the question. Although most of the questions are personal, don't neglect the scriptural foundation.

Question 14: Ask everyone to choose one way to begin to take good care of him or herself from the list of suggestions or something else God brings to mind.

Rebuilding

Ask: How did writing the letter to God help you with your situation with your homosexual or transgender loved one?

  What has God shown you so far about possible good from your situation?

Repeat Jeremiah 29:11 together, or ask a volunteer to say it aloud. Then ask two or three people to tell how this verse has helped them.

Close by praying together.

2
Encountering God

Purpose
To help group members learn to trust God in their situations with sexually broken loved ones.

Reflecting
Ask for responses to this question.

Then say: Many of the people we read about in Scripture dealt with staggering losses and heartbreaks as painful as the ones we face today. Job lost his ten children and all his possessions in a single day. Ruth's husband died, leaving her in poverty. David committed adultery and murder and faced the death of several beloved sons. And Paul suffered whippings and imprisonment at the hands of Roman soldiers. In fact, many of our heroes in the faith, including Nehemiah, experienced loneliness, disillusionment, and grief similar to what you may be facing right now.

Exploring
Question 1: Ask someone to read Nehemiah 1:4-6. After a volunteer answers this question, say: Nehemiah's prayer is similar to other prayers recorded in the Old Testament.

One at a time, ask four people to read the following prayers; then compare and contrast them with Nehemiah's.
- 1 Chronicles 17:16–27
- 2 Chronicles 20:5–12
- 2 Samuel 7:18–29
- Jonah 2:2–9

Ask: What did you learn about praying in the midst of your situation from these prayers?

Questions 4-9: Summarize the text, and discuss these questions.

Questions 10-11: If you have time, ask one or two people to read Psalm 139 aloud. If not, only ask for responses to the questions.

Questions 12-13: Discuss these questions. If you know you have unbelievers in the group, briefly explain the plan of salvation and encourage anyone who wants to know more or choose to accept Jesus as Savior from sin to talk with you after the meeting.

Rebuilding
Encourage everyone to repeat or read the Bible verse they chose to cling to and tell how it helped them. If you're short on time, ask for only two or three volunteers to respond.

Optional: Also repeat Psalm 4:1 together, or ask a volunteer to say it aloud. Then ask someone to tell how he or she used this verse this week.

Close the session with prayer.

3
Examining Our Guilt

Purpose
To help group members accept God's forgiveness of their sinful actions against their sexually broken loved ones and to extend forgiveness to them.

Reflecting
Read the opening anecdote, and discuss the question that follows it.

Exploring
Questions 1-5: Read the transition paragraph, then have someone read Nehemiah 1:5-7 and 11 aloud. Ask for responses to these questions.

Questions 6-8: You may want to skip these questions, depending on how open your group members have been with one another.

Question 10: Ask a volunteer to read these verses, then ask the question.

Say: God called David "a man after my own heart" (Acts 13:22). However, he was not above sinning. Have two group members read 2 Samuel 12:13 and 24:17-24.
   Ask: How did David respond when confronted with his sin?
   Discuss: How does your response compare with his? Why?

Question 14: Have someone read these verses from Psalm 103, then discuss the two questions.

Rebuilding
Summarize the paragraph under "Forgiving Our Loved Ones," and encourage group members to follow through with forgiving themselves and their loved ones.

Ask volunteers to read their letters to the group for feedback. Start with comments on what members like about a letter, then proceed to any constructive suggestions for improvement.

Repeat Psalm 32:5 together. Ask volunteers to tell how this verse helped them during the week.

Close with silent prayer, encouraging everyone to thank God for His forgiveness of their sins, ask for His help to forgive their homosexual or transgender loved ones, and show that forgiveness in meaningful ways.

4
Fearing Disclosure

Purpose
To help group members become comfortable with telling others about their loved ones' sexual brokenness, so they can receive prayer support and encouragement.

Reflecting
Optional: In advance, ask someone in the group who has a story similar to Susan's to tell it.

Discuss the three questions.

Exploring
Questions 1-10: Work through the Bible study and questions.

Question 11: One at a time, have someone read each verse before talking about how it impacts views of disclosure.

Questions 12-14, 16: Read the paragraph before question 12, then ask for responses to these questions.

Question 17: Briefly summarize Nehemiah's steps for approaching a difficult situation. Then ask group members to identify specific people they can go to for encouragement and prayer support.

Rebuilding
Ask volunteers to show and explain their relationship diagrams.

Read the following illustration:

> *A professor was giving a lecture to his student[s] on stress management. He raised a glass of water and asked the audience, "How heavy do you think this glass of water is?"*
>
> *The students' answers ranged from 20 to 500 grams.*
>
> *He smiled and said, "It does not matter on the absolute weight. It depends on how long you hold it. If I hold it for a minute, it is OK. If I hold it for an hour, I will have an ache in my right arm. If I hold it for a day, you will have to call an ambulance. It is the exact same weight, but the longer I hold it, the heavier it becomes.*
>
> *If we carry our burdens all the time, sooner or later, we will not be able to carry on, the burden becoming increasingly heavier. What you have to do is to put the glass down, rest for a while before holding it up again. We have to put down the burden periodically, so that we can be refreshed and are able to carry on (Malady of Art: Fear* by Jack White, Senkarik Publishing, 2010, p. 215).

Emphasize that we cannot carry the burden of our loved ones alone. That's why you have this group, as well as relationships with other people who will pray for and encourage you in this painful journey.

Repeat together Hebrews 3:13.

Divide your group into twos or threes. Have each person share one request related to disclosing a loved one's sexual preferences, then pray together for those requests. Encourage everyone to continue praying for the requests throughout the week.

5
Confronting Shame

Purpose
To help group members recognize false shame and learn how to gain freedom from it.

Reflecting
Read or summarize Denise's story.

Ask: What kind of shame did Denise experience as a result of her father's transgender desires?
  Why did her mother respond as she did?
  If shame has been part of your journey, describe the shame you've felt.

Exploring

Questions 1-3: Work through the Bible study and these questions.

Ask a couple of people to describe their observation of someone else's shame or embarrassment and tell how it is like theirs.

Questions 4-6: Read the Bible passages, and answer the questions.

Subjective shame: Explain this additional information.

Subjective shame begins in our childhood years. Unhealthy families instruct family members to repress their real emotions; to never talk about feelings, needs, or wants; to never make mistakes or, if they do, cover them up. They say things like:

- "You must always be in control, and do everything right. Success in life depends on performance and achievement."
- "Never trust anyone."
- "Never share family secrets."
- "Look good on the outside, and never share what's on the inside."
- "What will others think?"

Shame is generational. We have carried a sense of shame from our family of origin, going back many generations. Family secrets, as well as events and sins from the past, add to our subjective shame. Deeply held beliefs from childhood and shame-inducing experiences hide from our memories, making it difficult to remember them and making us resistant to change. Without realizing it or intending to do so, we can pass unhealthy, subjective shame to our children and grandchildren.

Questions 7-11: Discuss these questions about undeserved shame.

Ask: What has helped you cope with shame?

Be sensitive to the fact that some, many, or all of your group members have not yet learned to cope. If that's the case, spend a few minutes talking about how and why Jesus coped with shame.

Rebuilding

Ask a few volunteers to share their memory of a shameful situation and the Bible verse they chose to contradict it.

Repeat together Psalm 34:4-5, and talk about how these two verses helped group members on their journeys with sexually broken loved ones.

Close the session with prayer.

6
Inspecting the Brokenness

Purpose

To help group members realize God can use their brokenness to heal them and their homosexual or transgender loved ones.

Reflecting

If your group is at the point of trusting one another, go around the circle and ask group members to answer the question in this section and tell why they chose that number. Or ask for a few volunteers to share.

Exploring

Questions 1-14: Work through the Bible study and personal questions.

Question 4: Comment on what members' responses have in common or how they are all different. Point out that no matter what the painful issue, God understands and offers help and peace.

Question 6: You may want to ask everyone to respond, so the group can focus on the fact that relationships with sexually broken loves ones are not all full of pain.

Question 8: Ask the group to suggest specific actions for one another. Often other people have good ideas we might not think of.

Question 10: Sharing one another's words of hope from the Lord will encourage all group members, so allow enough time for responses. Those who don't have a word yet may find one in this discussion.

Questions 15-16: Skip these questions if you're short on time. If you do use them, realize that group members may be reluctant to answer.

Questions 17-18: Also skip these questions of you are short of time.

Rebuilding

If any group members had the conversation described in this section, have them tell what happened as a result and how they feel now about doing it. Encourage those who have not yet talked to their loved ones to follow through soon.

Repeat together Hosea 6:1-3, and talk about how this passage affected group members.

Close by reading Tozer's prayer, asking group members to pray it with you.

7
Preparing to Rebuild

Purpose
To help group members identify family characteristics that affect their relationships with sexually broken loved ones and take steps to change these characteristics.

Reflecting
Ask: When have you been ready to give up your faith because of the homosexuality or gender confusion of your loved one?

Exploring
Question 1: After someone reads Nehemiah 2:17-18 and group members respond, emphasize the fact that we can't do God's work alone. Neither can we rebuild our families alone; we need both God and other people to help us.

Questions 3-9: Discuss these questions.

Question 8: Have someone read "To Let Go." Go around the circle, asking everyone to name the statement that is most difficult to give up. Comment on how much your group has or doesn't have in common.

Question 10: One at a time, read the characteristics and ask for a show of hands from those who checked that item. Comment on how much group members have or don't have in common. Regardless, God is aware of what is going on in your families and wants to rebuild them.

Questions 11-13: Call for responses.

Question 14: Ask volunteers to identify which area they chose to work on first and what they are doing to change it. You may not get many responses, but that's okay.

Question 15: As people respond, ask them what is surprising about these revelations.

Question 17: Ask for responses to this question. You may want to develop plans for your group to educate your church or community. If so, set a separate time to meet for this purpose.

Rebuilding

Ask volunteers to report on which characteristic they researched and what they discovered.

Repeat Isaiah 38:17 together. Ask: How does this verse make you feel in light of your journey with your loved one?

Close with prayer.

8
Dealing with the Opposition

Purpose

To help group members identify the deceptions and temptations Satan uses to derail them from a relationship with their sexually broken loved ones and ways to overcome these tactics.

Reflecting

Discuss the two questions in this section.

Exploring

Question 1: After someone reads Nehemiah 4:1-3, ask the question.

    Optional: Explain that Sanballet and Tobiah are identified in Nehemiah as the major opponents to rebuilding the wall of Jerusalem. Both men were politically prominent in the area surrounding Jerusalem. Sanballet (a Babylonian name) held the position of governor over Samaria. Tobiah was thought to have been the governor of Transjordan.

    History tells us that Tobiah was a Jew. We can understand why Sanballet might have objected to the Jews rebuilding the walls, but why would Tobiah turn on his own people?

    In Ezra 4, we learn that an earlier attempt had been made to rebuild the walls after the Temple was rebuilt under Ezra. At that time, the officials and judges alerted Artaxerxes, the Persian king, through a letter that rebuilding Jerusalem's walls would affect the royal treasury: "The king should know that if this city is built and its walls are restored, no more taxes, tribute and duty will be paid, and eventually the royal revenues will suffer" (v. 13). They further informed him that he would be left with nothing if the walls were rebuilt (v. 16). Artaxerxes compelled them to stop.

Building the walls of Jerusalem could easily have been a threat to Sanballet and Tobiah's political status in the area. With the rebuilt Jerusalem, they might have lost financial benefits they were receiving from the Persian government. Pride and possessions appeared to be more important to them than achieving God's will.

Questions 2-6: Discuss these questions together.

Question 8: Ask a few volunteers to tell about their experiences talking with their homosexual or transgender loved ones about the questions listed before this one.

Questions 9-12: Discuss all or some of these questions.

If some of your group members still are not convinced homosexuality or transgenderism is sin, summarize or read these Bible passages and notes. Point out that in the original languages, such behavior is always addressed as ungodly:

- Genesis 19: the story of Sodom and Gomorrah. (You'll need to summarize the chapter.) Other passages, such as Jude 7, support the reason for Sodom and Gomorrah's punishment as "sexual immorality and perversion."
- Leviticus 18:22 and 20:13 explicitly prohibit a man having sex with a woman.
- Romans 1:18-32: Paul describes homosexual practice as part of the decadent society that God abandoned to sin.
- 1 Corinthians 6:9-11: Paul includes homosexuals in the list of sinners who will not inherit God's Kingdom. However, he also gives great hope for change: "And that is what some of you *were*" (emphasis added).

Question 15: Briefly summarize Tactic 1, and discuss this question.

Summarize: King David committed horrible sins in his life: adultery and murder. Yet when Nathan confronted him with his sin, he repented and asked for God's forgiveness. We have a choice to confess and repent of sin or allow it to take deeper root in our hearts.

It is true that Christians can struggle with homosexual and transgender feelings and attractions. These feelings or temptations are not chosen. However, we must also make the right moral choices to govern our lives and encourage our loved ones to do so too. Temptations come and go, but the choice of behaving in a sinful way determines who the person ultimately becomes. All of the combined feelings and temptations a person may have in a lifetime don't have the same ethical, moral, or legal weight as a single one of his or her actions.

Adam and Eve were not sinners because they dealt with temptations. They became sinners when they yielded to temptation and acted on it.

Questions 16-20: Discuss these questions, perhaps omitting the first question in #16.

Rebuilding

Point out the importance of the thought life in dealing with sexually broken loved ones. Then ask two or three people to relate their action plans and tell how these have helped.

Repeat Colossians 2:6-8 together, and ask one or two volunteers to tell how this passage impacted them during the week.

Close in prayer, or ask a volunteer to do so.

9
Fighting for Our Loved Ones

Purpose

To help group members move past discouragement with sexually broken loved ones and find prayer partners to support them as they seek to rebuild their families.

Reflecting

Ask the two questions in this section.

Exploring

Questions 1-4: Have someone read Nehemiah 4:7-17 aloud, then ask the questions.
Read the following quote from Warren W. Wiersbe to emphasize who the opposition is in the battle to rebuild our families:

> *The Christian's battle is not against flesh and blood, but against Satan and his demonic forces that use flesh and blood to oppose the Lord's work. If we hope to win the war and finish the work, we must use the spiritual equipment God has provided (Eph. 6:10-18; 2 Cor. 10:1-6). If we focus on the* visible *enemy alone and forget the* invisible *enemy, we are sure to start trusting our own resources; and this will lead to defeat (Be Determined, Colorado Springs, CO: David C. Cook, 1992, p. 64).*

Questions 5-6: Briefly talk about how discouraging it can be to deal with a family member who is sexually broken. Then discuss these questions.

Questions 8-16: Work through the four ways that kept Nehemiah forging ahead—prayer, persuasion, passion, and plan—by summarizing the text and discussing the questions.

Question 10: If you have time, you might want to role-play this situation to help members better know how to respond to such remarks. Ask one volunteer to be the parent and another one to call out ugly remarks he or she has heard about homosexual or transgender people. Have the parent respond in a gracious manner. Then ask for suggestions of other charitable ways to respond.

Question 12: Ask everyone to read or repeat the Bible verse they chose and, if willing, tell how it helped this week.

Question 16: Brainstorm ways group members can continue to support one another after this group study is over.

Rebuilding

Ask group members to tell what they learned from Nehemiah's plan.

Emphasize the importance of having prayer partners for this journey with loved ones, relating a time when having such partners helped you. Encourage everyone who does not have at least one partner to ask someone this week.

Repeat 1 Peter 5:8-9 together, and ask two volunteers to tell how these verses have impacted them.

Close with prayer, asking God to help your group resist Satan's temptations and stand firm in Him as they journey with their loved ones.

10
Putting on God's Armor

Purpose

To help group members understand and use the pieces of God's armor as they journey with their homosexual or transgender loved ones.

Reflecting

Read Jim's comments about homosexuality in this section. Then ask how group members responded to the comments and why.

Exploring

Questions 1-2: Mention that Nehemiah, too, was involved in spiritual warfare; and read Nehemiah 4:14. Ask volunteers to answer the questions.

Repeat or read together Ephesians 6:10-18.

Questions 3-10: Try to find a large picture of the armor Paul wrote about. (Ask your Sunday school superintendent, teachers, or church librarian for help.) Show the picture, briefly summarize each piece, and ask the questions. As you do so, be sure to connect the armor piece to the spiritual battle group members are in as they relate to their sexually broken loved ones.

Question 11: Instead of asking for a praise list, turn this question into a short sentence-prayer time by asking people to complete this sentence: "God, I praise You for ___." After a few minutes, close the prayer time.

Rebuilding

Discuss which piece of the armor is the most difficult one to wear and how to make it easier to put on.

Read "Just Keep Planting" by Adam Kahn:

> *Paul Rokich is my hero. When Paul was a boy growing up in Utah, he happened to live near an old copper smelter, and the sulfur dioxide that poured out of the refinery had made a desolate wasteland out of what used to be a beautiful forest.*
>
> *When a young visitor one day looked at this wasteland and saw that there was nothing living there—no animals, no trees, no grass, no bushes, no birds . . . nothing but fourteen thousand acres of black and barren land that even smelled bad—well, this kid looked at the land and said, "This place is crummy." Paul knocked him down. He felt insulted. But he looked around him and something happened inside him. He made a decision: Paul Rokich vowed that some day he would bring back the life to this land.*
>
> *Many years later Paul was in the area, and he went to the smelter office. He asked if they had any plans to bring the trees back. The answer was "No." He asked if they would let him try to bring the trees back. Again, the answer was "No." They didn't want him on their land.*
>
> *He realized he needed to be more knowledgeable before anyone would listen to him, so he went to college to study botany.*

At the college, he met a professor who was an expert in Utah's ecology. Unfortunately, this expert told Paul that the wasteland he wanted to bring back was beyond hope. He was told that his goal was foolish because even if he planted trees, and even if they grew, the wind would only blow the seeds forty feet per year, and that's all you'd get because there weren't any birds or squirrels to spread the seeds, and the seeds from those trees would need another thirty years before they started producing seeds of their own. Therefore, it would take approximately twenty thousand years to revegetate that six-square-mile piece of earth. His teachers told him it would be a waste of his life to try to do it. It just couldn't be done.

So he tried to go on with his life. He got a job operating heavy equipment, got married, and had some kids. But his dream would not die.

He kept studying up on the subject, and he kept thinking about it. And then one night he got up and took some action. He did what he could with what he had. . . .

Under the cover of darkness, he sneaked out into the wasteland with a backpack full of seedlings and started planting. For seven hours he planted seedlings.

He did it again a week later.

And every week, he made his secret journey into the wasteland and planted trees and shrubs and grass.

But most of it died.

For fifteen years he did this. When a whole valley of his fir seedlings burned to the ground because of a careless sheep-herder, Paul broke down and wept. Then he got up and kept planting.

Freezing winds and blistering heat, landslides and floods and fires destroyed his work time and time again. But he kept planting.

One night he found a highway crew had come and taken tons of dirt for a road grade, and all the plants he had painstakingly planted in that area were gone.

But he just kept planting.

Week after week, year after year he kept at it, against the opinion of the authorities, against the trespassing laws, against the devastation of road crews, against the wind and rain and heat ... even against plain common sense. He just kept planting.

Slowly, very slowly, things began to take root.

Then gophers appeared.

Then rabbits.

Then porcupines.

The old copper smelter eventually gave him permission, and later, as times were changing and there was political pressure to clean up the environment, the company actually hired Paul to do what he was already doing, and they provided him with machinery and crews to work with. Progress accelerated.

Now the place is fourteen thousand acres of trees and grass and bushes, rich with elk and eagles, and Paul Rokich has received almost every environmental award Utah has.

He says, "I thought that if I got this started, when I was dead and gone people would come and see it. I never thought I'd live to see it myself!"

It took him until his hair turned white, but he kept that impossible vow he made to himself as a child. . . .

The way you get something accomplished in this world is just to keep planting. Just keep working. Just keep plugging away at it one day at a time for a long time, no matter who criticizes you, no matter how long it takes, no matter how many times you fall.

Get back up again. And just keep planting.

Ask: How is Paul Rokich's situation similar to ours with our homosexual and transgender loved ones?

If no one mentions it, emphasize the need to persist. We can't give up praying for, talking with, and trusting God to work in their lives and to rebuild their families.

Close with prayer, thanking God for his unfailing love for both group members and loved ones and for how He has been working in your families. Express faith that He will continue to work in broken lives, even if you don't see immediate changes in their lifestyles.

LIVING STONES MINISTRIES

Creating opportunities for families impacted by sexual and relational brokenness to know God and thrive

Living Stones Ministries is a nonprofit, Christ-centered, nondenominational organization dedicated to helping families with issues of homosexuality and other forms of sexual brokenness. We are here to bring healing, to give hope, to be a redemptive resource for families filled with hurt and shame. Visit our website for a variety of media resources.

Living Stones Ministries is a member ministry of Restored Hope Network, "an inter-denominational membership governed network dedicated to restoring hope to those broken by sexual and relational sin, especially those impacted by homosexuality. We proclaim that Jesus Christ has life-changing power for all who submit to Christ as Lord; we also seek to equip His church to impart that transformation."

Living Stones Ministries takes its name from 1 Peter 2:4-5: "As you come to him, the living Stone—rejected by humans but chosen by God and precious to him—you also, like living stones, are being built into a spiritual house to be a holy priesthood, offering spiritual sacrifices acceptable to God through Jesus Christ."

Our Mission
- Introduce individuals and families to the loving and saving power of Jesus Christ.
- Proclaim the joy and fulfillment of a life lived in obedience to the teachings of God's Word.
- Provide safe places for individuals and families to openly share their grief and pain about homosexuality and other forms of sexual brokenness.
- Develop and distribute educational and inspirational materials.
- Educate churches, pastors, therapists, and other organizations through seminars, presentations, and conferences.
- Offer spiritual counseling and referrals for psychological counseling.

- Encourage the family of God to extend God's love and compassion to the sexually and relationally broken, to be Christ to one another.

Organizing a Support Group

If you are interested in organizing a support group for families and friends with issues of sexual brokenness, Living Stones Ministries has resources to assist you. Please contact us, and we will be happy to send them to you.

Living Stones Ministries
P.O. Box 1543
Glendora, CA 91740
626.963.6683
info@livingstonesministry.org
www.livingstonesministry.org

ORDER INFORMATION

REDEMPTION
PRESS

To order additional copies of this book, please visit
www.redemption-press.com.
Also available on Amazon.com and BarnesandNoble.com.
Or by calling toll free 1-844-2REDEEM.

CPSIA information can be obtained
at www.ICGtesting.com
Printed in the USA
FSHW02n1602041018
52596FS

9 781632 329011